Knowledge and understanding of the world

Sally Gray

Goals for the Foundation Stage

British Library Cataloguing-in-Publication Data A catalogue record for this book is available from the British Library.

ISBN 0 439 98353 3

Author
Sally Gray

Editor
Jane Bishop

Designer
Heather C Sanneh

Assistant Editor
Saveria Mezzana

Illustrations
Rebecca Archer

Series Designer
Clare Brewer

Cover photography
Derek Cooknell

Text © 2003 Sally Gray
© 2003 Scholastic Ltd

Designed using Adobe Pagemaker

Published by Scholastic Ltd,
Villiers House,
Clarendon Avenue,
Leamington Spa,
Warwickshire CV32 5PR

Visit our website at www.scholastic.co.uk
Printed by Proost NV, Belgium

1 2 3 4 5 6 7 8 9 0   3 4 5 6 7 8 9 0 1 2

Acknowledgements
Qualifications and Curriculum Authority for the use of extracts from the QCA/DfEE document *Curriculum Guidance for the Foundation Stage* © 2000 Qualifications and Curriculum Authority.
Every effort has been made to trace copyright holders and the publishers apologise for any inadvertent omissions.

The publishers gratefully acknowledge permission to reproduce the following copyright material: Jillian Harker for the use of 'Tale of two mice' and 'The coming of Raven' by Jillian Harker © 2003, Jillian Harker, both previously unpublished; Irene Yates for the use of 'The Three Little Pigs' and 'A busy day' by Irene Yates © 2003 Irene Yates, both previously unpublished.

Contents

Introduction   5

Planning   9

Assessment   15

Chapter 1   Exploration and investigation
Tried and tested   19
Collecting conkers   20
Sensory trail   21
All about animals   22
Bird garden   23
Wrapping up   24
Little shoppers   25
Colourful animals   26
Kitchen capers   27
Bath toys!   28

Chapter 2   Designing and making skills
Copy cats!   29
Cosy cottage   30
Huff and puff!   31
The inventors   32
Staircases   33
Let's make a book!   34
Caterpillar treats   35
A new toy   36
Scrapbooks   37
At the office   38

Chapter 3   Information and communication technology
ICT monitor   39
At the supermarket   40
The post office   41
Guess what it is!   42
Sound story   43
The listening area   44
Technology trail   45
Helping baby   46
Remote control   47
Finding out   48

Chapter 4   Sense of time
Yesterday   49
Sleeping Beauty   50

Goals for the Foundation Stage

Knowledge and understanding of the world

Grown-ups   51
Muddled up   52
Sharing time   53
The doctor's surgery   54
Achievement folders   55
Take one tree   56
When I was a baby   57
Days gone by   58

Chapter 5   Sense of place
It's a small world   59
Where shall we live?   60
What's it for?   61
Spotters   62
Town or country?   63
Word books   64
Litterbugs   65
Lots of pots   66
Favourite places   67
All kinds of homes   68

Chapter 6   Cultures and beliefs
Special events   69
Year scrapbook   70
Our group   71
African experience   72
Food from Mexico   73
World food festival   74
Multicultural tales   75
Raven's bag   76
International café   77
Traditional dress   78

Photocopiable pages
Planning – Daily activity sheet   79
Assessment – Exploration and investigation   80
Assessment – Designing and making, ICT   81
Assessment – Time, place, cultures and beliefs   82
Making a nest box   83
Animal patterns   84
The Three Little Pigs   85
Shape book   86
Make Teddy dance   87
A busy day   88
Spot the technology   89
After 100 years   90
My certificate   91
Tale of two mice   92
Where can you find them?   93
Where do you live?   94
Spicy salsa   95
The coming of Raven   96

Introduction

© 2001, COMSTOCK, INC

The aims of this series

This book forms part of a series of six books, *Goals for the Foundation Stage*, written to support the teaching of the Early Learning Goals as described in *Curriculum Guidance for the Foundation Stage* (QCA). Each book in the series comprehensively covers one of the six Areas of Learning.

The ideas suggested can be applied equally well to the documents on pre-school education published for Scotland, Wales and Northern Ireland.

Each of the books in the series provides an up-to-date, comprehensive and invaluable practical guide to teaching the individual Areas of Learning. Each book contains an introduction, a chapter on planning, a chapter on assessment, an activity chapter for each cluster of the relevant Early Learning Goals, and a set of versatile photocopiable sheets (some linked to planning and assessment, and some activity sheets).

The books can be used in a flexible way. The set may be used as a Foundation Stage curriculum package, or the books be used separately, alongside your usual activities and planning and assessment methods. The individual books may be used in their entirety to plan and broadly cover all aspects of the Area of Learning, or they can simply be used to supplement existing work in a variety of group settings.

Covering the Goals

This book, *Knowledge and Understanding of the World*, contains six activity chapters – one for each cluster of Early Learning Goals in this Area of Learning. This ensures that, across the book, there is full and even coverage of this Area of Learning. Practitioners will find the activities an invaluable source of new and exciting ideas that can be followed methodically or dipped into at any time throughout the year. The chapters are:

■ Chapter 1 – Exploration and investigation. This chapter provides ten activities (one per page) linked to the four Early Learning Goals in this cluster. The children will be involved in a wide range of experiences, such as taking part in a sensory trail around your setting ('Sensory trail' on page 21), planning and creating a bird garden ('Bird garden' on page 23) and testing and examining bath toys ('Bath toys!' on page 28).

Introduction

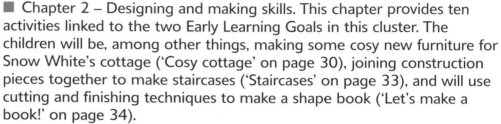

■ Chapter 2 – Designing and making skills. This chapter provides ten activities linked to the two Early Learning Goals in this cluster. The children will be, among other things, making some cosy new furniture for Snow White's cottage ('Cosy cottage' on page 30), joining construction pieces together to make staircases ('Staircases' on page 33), and will use cutting and finishing techniques to make a shape book ('Let's make a book!' on page 34).

■ Chapter 3 – Information and communication technology. This chapter provides ten activities linked to the Early Learning Goal in this cluster. From showing an interest in ICT to operating simple equipment and completing a simple program on a computer, the activities in this chapter give suggestions for progressing towards this Early Learning Goal. For example, the children will use equipment to record sounds in 'Sound story' on page 43, and they will learn to manipulate simple technological toys in 'Helping baby' on page 46.

■ Chapter 4 – Sense of time. This chapter provides ten activities linked to the Early Learning Goal in this cluster. Through a wide range of exciting ideas, the children will be encouraged to remember and talk about significant things that have happened to them ('Yesterday' on page 49), begin to differentiate between past and present ('Sleeping Beauty' on page 50), show an interest in the lives of people familiar to them ('Muddled up' on page 52) and remember and talk about significant things that have happened to them ('The doctor's surgery' on page 54).

■ Chapter 5 – Sense of place. This chapter provides ten activities linked to the two Early Learning Goals in this cluster. Activities such as 'Where shall we live?' on page 60, in which the children use a playmat to make and plan an imaginary town, help them to develop an interest in the world that they live in. They are also encouraged to talk about the features of the environment that they like and dislike, with activities such as 'Litterbugs' on page 65 and 'Favourite places' on page 67.

■ Chapter 6 – Cultures and beliefs. This chapter provides ten activities linked to the Early Learning Goal in this cluster. The lively activities found here cover a range of Stepping Stones in progression towards achieving the Early Learning Goal. For example, in 'Special events' on page 69, the children will be encouraged to share their feelings about a significant personal event; they will listen to some African music in 'African experience' on page 72, and they will help to set up a role-play café in 'International café' on page 77, in order to gain an awareness of the cultures and beliefs of others.

Knowledge and understanding of the world

Using this book

Each of the sixty activities in this book follows a standard format, starting with the Stepping Stone and Early Learning Goal covered by the activity.

The Stepping Stones for each activity are colour-coded with activities at the simplest level shaded yellow, those in the middle shaded blue and the more difficult shaded green, to match the colours used to show progression in the document *Curriculum Guidance for the Foundation Stage*.

Each activity includes the size of the group, any resources required and a step-by-step, bullet-pointed explanation of how to complete the activity, including suggestions for support and extension provided as the final two statements in 'What to do'.

A section of 'More ideas' suggests further ways to achieve the same learning objectives, and a section on other curriculum areas shows how the same skills can be covered across other Areas of Learning. Lastly, a 'Home links' section provides suggestions for linking with the children's home environment.

The photocopiable sheets

A collection of 18 photocopiable sheets at the end of this book provides additional support. The first sheet, on page 79, links to the Planning chapter and is intended to be used as a template for a detailed activity plan. It is not suggested that such a plan be completed for every activity that is carried out in your setting; however, you may find it useful when planning an informal or formal assessment, when several adults will be completing the activity with different groups of children and you wish to maintain a consistent approach, or as a checklist for yourself during a busy session. The activities that you record on this sheet may be used over again and can form part of an activity reference file for you to return to, term after term.

The next three photocopiable sheets link to the Assessment chapter, and their use is explained on page 18.

The remaining fourteen photocopiable sheets are linked to the six activity chapters in this book, with two or three accompanying sheets for each chapter. Some of the sheets are intended for the children to work with, such as a template for making a shape book on page 86, or a picture of Sleeping Beauty's castle to discuss on page 90. Others are stories linked to the activities, such as 'The Three Little Pigs' on page 85, or 'The coming of Raven' on page 96. Others still provide useful adult reference material, such as the instructions for making a bird box on page 83, or the recipe for salsa on page 95.

Links with other curriculum areas

As an early years practitioner, you will know that, although the curriculum is divided into distinct Areas of Learning and you apply a certain focus to the activities that you provide for the children in your care, all aspects of learning for young children – whether personal, social and emotional development, mathematical or physical development – are interrelated.

Although this book focuses on activities specifically designed to enable progression towards the Early Learning Goals for Knowledge and understanding of the world, the children will also be using creative, social, physical, mathematical and literary skills. For example, the activities in Chapter 6 provide opportunities for the children to find out about their own cultures and beliefs and those of others, and they will be exploring their feelings (linked closely to the Area of Learning for Personal, social and emotional development) and learning to express themselves (linked closely to Communication, language and literacy).

For each activity in this book you will find a section entitled 'Other curriculum areas', in which there are further ways to achieve the same Stepping Stone or Early Learning Goal through other Areas of Learning.

Links with home

It is now well recognised that learning for children in the early years is most effective when a strong partnership between home and practitioners exists. Parents and carers are invaluable sources of information about their children's needs and capabilities, and children benefit greatly if there is an element of consistency in the expectations and approaches found in both their homes and their learning environments.

Each of the 60 activities in this book includes a section on ways to involve parents and carers in their children's learning. These suggestions include inviting parents and carers in to your setting as helpers, visitors and experts. Other 'Home links' ideas suggest sending home stories and activity sheets for the children to share with their parents or carers, and others encourage the children to share news and objects brought in from home with the rest of the children.

By providing a bridge for each child between their home and your group, you will be boosting the children's confidence and success.

© SODA

Planning

Why plan?

Comprehensive planning is the most effective way to ensure that the children in your setting receive a balanced, broad, stimulating and individualised learning programme.

At the outset of each planning cycle, and especially for those new to the processes of detailed planning, the task may seem onerous and challenging. However, over time – as you learn the needs of the children, establish good working relationships with colleagues and carers and become increasingly familiar with the curriculum – planning will become less daunting and will eventually save you time, presenting you with rich rewards.

© TOM HURST/SODA

Carefully recorded plans may be used over again and, depending on the depth of detail of the written plans, they may be passed on to other colleagues to use with targeted groups or individuals. Planning records can also be made available to parents and carers in the form of charts or newsletters, or on notice-boards.

Purpose of planning

Plans have a number of uses. Some of the main ones are:
- to ensure even and balanced coverage of the curriculum
- to share information with others
- to record the children's experiences, interest and progress
- to act as a checklist in the middle of a busy session
- to ensure continuity as the children change or move on to different settings
- to enable you to maximise the potential of learning opportunities and also unexpected situations
- to ensure that the individual needs of all the children in your setting are met and that their potential is realised.

Teamwork and planning

Many people working with young children are in situations where there is a team of adults working together. If this is the case, communication between all those working with the children is an essential part of the planning process. Where possible, it is important to have regular meetings to ensure that all concerned have shared goals and that they are working in similar ways to achieve learning goals and to support the needs of the children. These regular meetings also serve to provide valuable feedback on activities, including observations of individual and group needs.

Knowledge and understanding of the world

These observations will feed back into the planning process, and daily or short-term plans can be modified to reflect the growing knowledge of the children's needs and capabilities. Many settings find it useful to assign key workers to specific children, in order to ensure that each child receives appropriate attention and is monitored and observed on a regular basis.

If you work alone, perhaps as a childminder with a small group of children, it is a good idea to try to establish a network of other people working in similar situations, in order to share notes and ideas as part of your professional development.

Links with observation and assessment
Planning and assessment are inextricably linked aspects of work with early years children. For example, it is important to plan regular formal assessments of the children's progress. Conversely, as informal assessments take place, you will notice areas of the children's learning that require extra support, whether in terms of extension or reinforcement, and these will need to be incorporated into your daily or weekly planning. Once more, this highlights the importance of teamwork and regular feedback sessions as part of your planning process.

The Foundation Stage
In planning to meet the requirements of the Foundation Stage curriculum, the document *Curriculum Guidance for the Foundation Stage* will almost certainly be an important tool. Each of the six identified Areas of Learning is broken down in a number of ways – aspects of learning (such as 'Exploration and investigation' for Knowledge and understanding of the world), Early Learning Goals and Stepping Stones (on the way to reaching the Goals). This breakdown of the curriculum can be used to good effect to ensure even and progressive curriculum coverage when setting out long-term plans.

In this book, you will find a chapter to cover each aspect of learning for the area of Knowledge and understanding of the world. Within each chapter, there are activities that are linked to each of the Early Learning Goals for that aspect of learning, as well as wide coverage of many of the Stepping Stones along the way to reaching the Goals. The activities have been written to include possible adaptations to support and extend the learning. You can therefore easily use this book alongside your plans to help meet your planned learning intentions.

Long-, medium- and short-term planning
A long-term plan acts as an overview for up to a year ahead, showing the opportunities that will be offered to the children. It broadly sets out what you intend the children to learn and will cover all areas of the curriculum.

A short-term plan is based on the long-term plan and is also developed with ongoing observation and assessment of the children. It covers in more specific detail what you intend the children to learn and how you aim to achieve this. It is usually drawn up on a daily or weekly basis (or both). Both types of plan are intended as guides and should not be followed rigidly, allowing scope to pursue unplanned events and to capture and maximise upon the children's obvious enjoyment and interest of things that occur, or that they notice.

Medium-term plans are sometimes made to fill in the gaps between the two main types of plan, and are used less frequently.

© DAVID MAGER/SODA

Equal opportunities

The plans that you make for your setting must take into account any special educational and physical needs of the children in your care. This will include anything from providing the right kind of scissors for left-handed children, to ensuring access to all areas of your room for wheelchair users, as well as planning specific activities for children with identified special educational needs. This type of planning will be undertaken in consultation with parents, carers, support workers, colleagues and your SENCO (Special Educational Needs Co-ordinator), where appropriate.

Planning should also ensure that children from all ethnic groups are given equal opportunities. Positive images of children and adults from a wide range of ethnic backgrounds and cultures can help to promote effective learning and will be of benefit to all the children in your group. The activities in Chapter 6 of this book ('Cultures and beliefs') will help to support this work.

It is also vitally important that children of both sexes are given equal opportunities and access to all the play and learning areas in your setting.

Knowledge and understanding of the world

This book can be used to help towards the long- and short-term planning for the particular Area of Learning for Knowledge and understanding of the world. As part of your short-term planning, you could pick and choose some of the activities. For example, if your focus for in a particular week happens to be 'Exploration and investigation', you may like to choose from the activities in Chapter 1. Similarly, if some of the children in your setting are experiencing the arrival of new siblings, you may like to take the opportunity to do some of the activities related to babies, such as 'Tried and tested' on page 19 or 'Helping baby' on page 46.

Alternatively, you may use the book to aid your long-term planning. You could do this by focusing on a chapter of the book for each half-term of the year and completing most of the activities, supplemented by other activities of your own choice linked to your particular topics, and from your knowledge of the children's strengths and interests.

Creating a rich learning environment

As well as planning a rich range of activities to teach and support learning in the area of Knowledge and understanding of the world, it is important to ensure that you make plans to maximise the potential of the learning environment itself. Young children spend a great deal of time engaged in free play in the early years, and by providing suitable resources and a stimulating environment you will be helping to lead their play to ensure that it is purposeful and fulfilling.

In the Area of Learning for Knowledge and understanding of the world, children are developing the skills, knowledge and understanding that will help them to make sense of the world that surrounds them. It is vital that children are immersed in an environment that stimulates their interest and curiosity. The following suggestions are linked either to traditional play areas or other organisational features of an early years setting, and will help you to plan for a stimulating and effective environment.

Organisation of your setting

Clearly labelled equipment that is stored in a regular place and kept clean and accessible to all the children is of paramount importance when planning your learning environment. Check the contents of your storage boxes regularly and encourage the children to help you sort through equipment. This in itself will promote the exploration and investigation skills associated with this Area of Learning.

The interest table

Set up an interest table on a permanent basis in your room. It could be linked to your current topic, for example, 'Homes', and you could place

on it materials such as bricks, straw, household fabrics and so on. Alternatively, you may choose a seasonal focus such as 'Festivals' or 'Seasons'. The most important thing is to make sure that the contents of the table are changed regularly, to captivate the children's interest and to hold their attention. If possible, attach a backing board to the table, so that you can display items related to your theme.

Draw the children's attention to the table each time you change the contents. Set challenges for the children to investigate on the table, and provide them with the necessary equipment and resources so that they can meet the challenges.

The book or story corner

Make your book corner a stimulating place by putting up special themed displays and posters linked to your current topic. Introduce some multi-sensory cushions to adorn the area, as well as the children's own made puppets and models linked to stories and your current topic. Place these on a low table for the children to choose during free play.

Books should, of course, not be confined just to the traditional story corner in your setting. Make sure that an abundance of books on themes linked to this Area of Learning, such as books about festivals, seasons and weather, and a wide range of story-books and information books permeate your setting. For example, in a role-play area set up as a veterinary clinic, you could include information books about animals.

© SCOTT CAMPBELL/SODA

The role-play area
A well-stocked and imaginative role-play area is a key part of any early years setting. Imaginary play extends across all curriculum boundaries, developing the children's social and communication skills, and enriching all other aspects of their early development. By providing a range of interesting resources in the role-play area, you can encourage the children to explore and investigate objects, events and materials.

A traditional home corner, for example, may contain a range of child-friendly kitchen devices, a telephone, DIY equipment and so on. There are a number of activities within this book that focus on the use of the role-play area, for example, 'Little shoppers' on page 25, 'At the office' on page 38 and 'The doctor's surgery' on page 54.

The listening area
For some suggestions for ways to enhance the listening area in your setting, see the activity 'The listening area' on page 44.

The art and craft area
One of the busiest places in an early years setting is the art and craft area, and a well-organised space can result in some wonderfully creative free play. Ideas for setting up the area to maximise the potential for learning in the area of Knowledge and understanding of the world include providing an 'Inventor's' box or designated area (see the activity 'The inventors' on page 32). This can be a collection of reclaimed materials, some suggestion cards (either models to copy or one-line suggestions, such as 'Make a chocolate tester'!) and access to a range of

Knowledge and understanding of the world

equipment and resources, for example, paper, card, sticky tape, glue sticks, safety scissors and so on (the accessibility of this kind of equipment needs to be in keeping with your setting's health and safety guidelines).

Providing a 'treasure box' is another way to promote learning in this area. Cover an old cardboard box with a lid in some shiny paper and label it 'Treasure box'. Fill the box with a range of materials in a variety of textures and colours. Allow the children to explore the contents freely and encourage them to use these for some colourful collage pictures or to adorn models made in the Inventor's area!

Small-world and construction play

Occasionally, set up an interest table devoted to one of the children's favourite small-world play or construction sets, perhaps to suit a particular theme. Set up a small-world environment and encourage the children to interact with it by regularly introducing some scenarios, such as the scene of an accident, the building of a new school or row of shops, or a natural disaster such as a flood!

© PHOTODISC VIA SODA

Sand, water and malleable materials

Ensure that you have a range of tools and equipment to use in the areas of sand and water play, and for use with malleable materials. You do not need to spend a fortune – household equipment such as funnels, jugs, beakers and bowls are excellent resources for sand and water play. Plastic, blunt knives, forks and spoons can be used creatively with malleable materials.

Outdoor play

An outdoor area at your setting is a wonderful resource in itself. Encourage the children to use it in a number of ways by planning it as carefully as you would the inside setting.

Set up quiet, shady areas with nature books and equipment such as binoculars and magnifying glasses, or create a wildlife area by setting a bird table or garden (see 'Bird garden' on page 23).

Provide role-play equipment such as dressing-up clothes, signposts and road layouts for the children to use with outdoor equipment and wheeled vehicles, or consider theming a 'Wendy house' to be, for example, a seaside beach hut, a bird hide or a newspaper kiosk.

Also, encourage the children to explore the environment for supervised free play.

Knowledge and understanding of the world

Assessment

Why assess?
The process of carefully assessing and monitoring children as they move through the Foundation Stage is an essential part of the work of early years practitioners. But why is it so important and who benefits from the process? Here are some of the reasons to maintain a well-structured assessment programme in your setting.

© 2001, COMSTOCK, INC

Curriculum coverage
Thorough assessment records can be referred back to throughout the year, acting as a check that key curriculum areas have been covered in detail.

Suitability of activities
Regular observation and assessment of the children will feed into the planning process, to ensure the suitability of the activities that you carry out with them. By assessing the children on a regular basis, you can plan activities that are suited to their individual needs and strengths.

Shared information
Carefully kept assessment records provide important information for other practitioners if the child is moving to a new setting. Assessment records can be carried forward with the child as they progress through their schooling. This transfer of relevant information will help to prevent gaps from forming in a child's learning and will save the child's new teacher wasting time covering ground already sufficiently covered.

Involving parents and carers
The best assessment records are completed with a degree of parental (or other significant carers') involvement. Parents are obviously the most important source of information about how a child is achieving at home. Some of the questions that you may ask are, 'Is the child fluent in any other languages?', 'What are their main interests?' and 'Are they proficient in using a computer in the home?'. A two-way partnership with carers will enrich your planning and subsequent assessment. It is vital, too, to keep them informed of their child's progress, especially if you have any concerns. Carefully documented assessment records can be shared at regular intervals.

Special educational needs
A well-planned and well-documented assessment programme is a crucial tool in the early identification of special educational needs. The assessment

Knowledge and understanding of the world

© JAMES LEVIN/SODA

process itself may draw your attention to a child's needs. The written records of the identified need, the action taken and the progress made, will provide essential documentation to present to support agencies and workers, as well as the child's carers. Early identification of special educational needs can help to make a difference to the eventual outcome of the child's learning progress.

Check your methods

A thorough assessment programme will enable practitioners to reflect on their own performance. If the majority of children in your care are progressing satisfactorily through the Stepping Stones to the Early Learning Goals, then it is likely that your methods and practice are being effective. If, however, it becomes apparent as a result of your assessments that there are gaps in the children's learning, then you will be able to adjust your programme accordingly. Such reflection is an important part of ongoing professional development for the practitioners and their staff.

Surprise results

Sometimes assessments can bring forward some surprises. A particular child may be stronger in a certain area than you had realised, or a child may not have fully grasped a concept in which you had assumed they were competent. Such surprises can then be dealt with by feeding assessment findings into the planning process. In such a way it is possible to keep pace with the children's progress, needs and development.

Working with others

As indicated in the section above, it is of paramount importance that practitioners work alongside parents, carers, colleagues and support workers and agencies to build up a complete picture of each child's progress and development. This communication is essential, not only in terms of planning appropriate work for the children, but also to ensure continuity of practice between all the adults that are working with the children, whether at home or in the learning environment.

By passing on and sharing knowledge of a child's strengths and capabilities, as well as areas for special support or encouragement, you can be positive that the child will receive appropriate intervention and guidance as they progress through the Foundation Stage and into Key Stage 1.

Knowledge and understanding of the world

Types of assessment

Without realising it, most practitioners are in the process of assessing the children that they work with throughout the session or day. They listen to children's responses and probe for further information, finding out how much more they know. They spontaneously modify an activity when it is clear that a child is ready to go further or requires extra support. This type of assessment could be regarded as an aspect of informal assessment. Informal assessment in its purest form is slightly more premeditated and contrived, but is, as its name suggests, a relaxed, unobtrusive way to monitor a child's progress.

Informal assessment

Your observations of the children as they complete or take part in a range of activities are likely to form the basis for most of your informal assessment. Practitioners will find a number of ways to achieve this type of assessment. They may, for example, choose one or two activities across the course of a week and assign the children's key workers to make observations as they work alongside the children during the specified activities.

Alternatively, practitioners might choose to focus on a group of children across the course of a session, day or week and take notes about all the activities in which they take part. However you decide to do it, a systematic approach is the best way to ensure that you obtain enough relevant information about each of the children in your care.

Formal assessment

On the other hand, more formal assessments will usually take place at a specific point in time (for example, at the end of each term) and these are usually conducted as a specific activity. Formal assessment is frequently used to check whether a certain skill (Stepping Stone or Early Learning Goal) has been achieved.

In January 2003, the Qualifications and Curriculum Authority introduced a new assessment document for early years practitioners working within the Foundation Stage. The *Foundation Stage Profile* provides a 12-page document to be completed for each child throughout the Foundation Stage. Within it, the curriculum is broken down to provide assessment for all six Areas of Learning, with nine 'targets' for Knowledge and understanding of the world.

© JOHN FORTUNATO/SODA

Putting the child at ease

Whichever type of assessment you are undertaking with the children, it is very important that they are put at their ease at all times. Children will have to face enough exam

Knowledge and understanding of the world

pressures later in their lives, without having to deal with the pressure to perform at such a young age. Informal assessments need not be apparent at all. Hopefully the children will be used to you scribbling notes, perhaps when you do some shared writing together or as you demonstrate writing for a number of purposes, such as memos, notes to parents and carers, writing comments in their reading records and so on.

It is more difficult to be discreet during formal assessments, but this should still be possible, if you keep the pace relaxed and behave naturally. Remember to provide lots of encouragement and give plenty of positive feedback. Whenever you feel that a child is wary, nervous or agitated in some way, it is best to halt the procedure and start afresh another time.

Assessment and the Foundation Stage curriculum

The document *Curriculum Guidance for the Foundation Stage* provides assessment guidance throughout. It aims to help practitioners assess by identifying 'examples of what children do' alongside the Stepping Stones and Early Learning Goals. These examples, in familiar set-ups, help practitioners to identify when knowledge, skills and understanding have been achieved by the children in their settings. This informal assessment of the children feeds in to future planning.

Using this book for assessment

The three assessment photocopiable sheets on pages 80, 81 and 82 may be used to record your notes and observations. Across the three sheets there is a section devoted to each of the Early Learning Goals for this Area of Learning. There is a space provided next to each Goal, in which you can make notes from a formal or informal assessment. Make sure that you allow plenty of settling-in time to your setting before you make any formal assessments of a child. You may decide to carry out an assessment and then to add further notes at future dates to the same sheet. Alternatively, make multiple copies of the sheets to make separate assessments on each child throughout the Foundation Stage.

Remember to include any special information about individual children and to record how frequent their grasp of a certain skill is, as some children remember how to complete a task one day and appear to have lost the very same skill another! Remember to include information about the level of adult support needed to achieve a certain objective.

The three assessment sheets will provide you with a checklist of the work covered with the children as well as a record of their progress towards each of the Goals. The sheets may be used flexibly – for example, you may wish to focus on certain Goals and take notes three times across the year, with less emphasis on Goals that a child has achieved during the early part of the year.

Alongside the *Foundation Stage Profile*, the sheets will be a useful reference to hand on to the children's next setting, or for discussion with parents, carers and other adults who work with the children.

© CLARA VON AICH/SODA

Young children are naturally curious and hungry for information. This chapter provides ideas to encourage their exploration and investigation skills using a range of resources and information sources, both indoors and outdoors.

Tried and tested

What to do

■ Ask the children to remember the sorts of toys that they used to play with when they were babies or toddlers. Have any of the children got younger brothers or sisters? What do they play with?

■ Show the children the selection of baby and toddler toys. Let them explore them freely. Encourage them to talk about what they are doing.

■ Now ask the children to take turns to select one of the toys. What have they found out about it? What is it made of? How does it work? Talk about the toy together.

■ Next invite the children to pass the toy around the group, letting each child investigate its properties. Is the toy suitable for a baby? Why do they think so?

■ Ask younger children to concentrate on two or three toys only. Suggest that they demonstrate how the toy works if they are finding it hard to describe it.

■ Let older children sort the toys, firstly to your specified criteria, such as plastic toys and wooden toys. Then ask them to sort the toys to a criteria of their own choice. How have they sorted them?

More ideas

■ Have a spring clean of the toys in your setting. Help the children to sort the toys and put them away tidily.

■ Design and make a simple safe toy for a baby or toddler.

■ Encourage the children to each bring in a favourite toy to talk about at circle time.

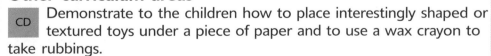

Other curriculum areas

CD Demonstrate to the children how to place interestingly shaped or textured toys under a piece of paper and to use a wax crayon to take rubbings.

PD Let the children explore some large wheeled toys before using them in outdoor play.

Collecting conkers

Stepping Stone
Describe simple features of objects and events.

Early Learning Goal
Investigate objects and materials by using all of their senses as appropriate.

Group size
Whole group.

What you need
Sufficient adult helpers; sorting (or seed) trays.

What to do
■ Let parents and carers know that you will be taking the children for a walk, and obtain the necessary consents. Arrange for extra adult helpers to accompany you on the day (check Local Authority guidelines).
■ Go for an autumnal walk with the children. Ask them to use their senses of sight, hearing and touch to explore the autumn environment – for example, listening to the sound of leaves crunching underfoot.

■ Gather some autumn materials to take back to your room, such as fallen leaves, twigs and conkers.
■ Back in your setting, divide the children into groups, with an adult helper each, and provide each group with a bag of autumn objects. Ask the children to sort the objects into different sets by placing them in the separate trays.
■ Let each group decide, with adult guidance, how they will sort their objects. Encourage them to use their different senses, such as sorting by colour (sight) and by texture (touch).
■ Share the different groups' findings at circle time. Encourage the children to describe what they have found out.
■ Help younger children to sort the objects into specified sets, such as leaves, conkers and twigs.
■ Invite older children to help you to make a table-top display of the autumn objects, then label the display with the children's own words and descriptions.

More ideas
■ Ask the children to paint pictures of themselves on the walk and add these, as well as the objects that they collected, to a wall frieze to make a multi-sensory, 3-D autumn display.
■ Place some of the objects inside a feely bag. Ask the children to take it in turns to put their hands inside the bag, feel an object and try to describe it to the rest of the group. Can the others guess what it is?

Other curriculum areas
CD Make some simple music shakers by filling empty tubs with the autumn objects.
MD Use the conkers for size and comparison work. Line them up in order of size and let older children weigh them to find out which is the heaviest.

Sensory trail

What to do

■ Explain to the children that you will be asking them to find some things as they walk around the room. Tell them that they will be using all their senses as they go on the trail.

■ Concentrate on one sense at a time.

■ Start with the sense of sight. Challenge the children to each find, for example, a red object as they walk around the room.

■ Ask the children to report back to you, bringing their objects.

■ Now continue the game, this time concentrating on a different sense. For example, ask the children to find something that they can rattle (for hearing).

■ Carry on the game with the sense of touch, asking the children to find something smooth, rough or scrunchy.

■ Go with the children to investigate objects by the sense of smell. Focus on two or three everyday items, such as soap, and the children's plimsolls!

■ Finish by inviting the children to come and taste some food and drink at snack time. Check for any food allergies and dietary requirements first.

■ Let younger children work in pairs with an adult. Use the opportunity to help to develop their descriptive vocabulary.

■ Make the task more challenging for older children by asking them to find several things for each sense. Encourage them to make some suggestions for things that they might look for.

More ideas

■ Let each child collect a set of objects from around the room and put them in a bag. Ask them to show you their objects, saying which sense they used most when they found each one.

■ Play a version of 'Kim's game', putting five or six objects on a tray and describing them to the children. Cover the objects with a cloth and ask the children to try to remember what they were. Give descriptive clues to help them remember.

Other curriculum areas

PD Ask the children to explore a selection of malleable materials and tools. Encourage them to describe how the materials feel and how they are manipulating them.

MD Gather all the children's collections of objects together and use them for sorting activities.

Stepping Stone
Show curiosity and interest by facial expression, movement or sound.

Early Learning Goal
Investigate objects and materials by using all of their senses as appropriate.

Group size
Three to four children.

What you need
Just the children.

Home links
Suggest that parents and carers help their children to take a sensory trail around a chosen room at home.

All about animals

Stepping Stone
Examine objects and living things to find out more about them.

Early Learning Goal
Find out about, and identify, some features of living things, objects and events they observe.

Group size
Whole group, then small groups or individuals.

What you need
Story-books, information books, posters, photographs and CD-ROMs about animals; paper; colouring and drawing materials; adult helper (confident in the use of a computer).

Home links
Ask if any parents or carers are able to come in on a regular basis to work with the children on the group's computer. Offer to provide training if necessary.

What to do
■ Over a period of time, read lots of stories featuring animals to the children. After each story, talk to the children about the animal featured. What do they know about the animal? What do they like about it? How can they find out more?

■ Make a display of the books that you have read in the story corner. Add some information books that feature the same animals, and display posters and photographs near by.

■ Now work with individuals or small groups and take them to your story corner. Draw their attention to the books and the display, and ask them to choose their favourite animal.

■ Help them to use the books to find out all they can about their chosen animal. Talk about what the animal looks like, what it likes to eat, where it lives and so on.

■ Suggest that the children each draw a picture of their chosen animals.

■ Help younger children to write a simple caption for their pictures.

■ Let older children take turns, with an adult helper, to use the computer to find out some more about their chosen animal, using CD-ROMs or the Internet.

More ideas
■ Ask individual children to tell you what they have found out. Scribe their words on to the back of their pictures. Help them to show their work at circle time.

■ Compile the children's work into an 'All about animals' group book.

■ Build up a list of useful websites that feature animals. Print off some of the material to make a scrapbook to go in the story corner.

Other curriculum areas

PD	Make models of the children's chosen animals, using malleable materials such as Plasticine.
CD	Learn some animal action rhymes and develop movements to go with them.

Bird garden

Early Learning Goal
Find out about, and identify, some features of living things, objects and events they observe.

Group size
Whole group.

What you need
The photocopiable sheet 'Making a nest box' on page 83 (optional); bird food; bird table; gardening tools; soil and pots (or borders); selection of plants and creepers.

Preparation
If outdoor space is limited, add some plants such as sweet violets and primroses in pots, or sunflowers in a grow bag.
If you have borders, plant a range of shrubs that will attract birds, and also provide them with nesting cover (ideas include lavender, lilac and aubretia). Make sure that the plants and shrubs that you choose are not poisonous.

What to do

■ Explain to the children that you are trying to encourage birds to visit your outdoor area. Ask them if any birds visit their gardens or window sills at home.

■ Help the children to think about the things that birds need, such as food and shelter.

■ Ask them for suggestions of things that you can do to help the birds, such as providing bird food and a bird bath. Tell them your ideas, too.

■ Put out a bird table and food.

■ The photocopiable sheet provides instructions for making a nest box. You may wish to make one of these and install it as part of the grand opening of your bird-friendly outdoor area!

■ Encourage younger children to look out for any birds that visit your outdoor area.

■ Involve older children in planting the new plants and in creating the bird garden.

More ideas

■ Make your own bird food by melting lard and mixing in some bird seed and dried fruit. Turn it out on to a bird table when hardened.

■ Hold a garden party to celebrate your new bird garden.

Other curriculum areas

CLL Use information books to find out about birds that commonly visit people's gardens.

MD Keep a tally of the number of birds that visit your new bird garden.

Home links

Ask for volunteers to follow the instructions on the photocopiable sheet to make a nesting box for the group. Give out copies of the sheet for parents and carers to make one for their own gardens.

Knowledge and understanding of the world

Wrapping up

Stepping Stone
Examine objects and living things to find out more about them.

Early Learning Goal
Find out about, and identify, some features of living things, objects and events they observe.

Group size
Two to four children.

What you need
A selection of objects such as some photographs, a china cup or ornament, some cakes or chocolates, and some clothes; range of packing material such as brown paper, padded envelopes, tissue paper, stiff card and bubble wrap (use under adult supervision); sticky tape; scissors.

What to do
■ Ask the children if they have ever received a parcel in the post.
■ Tell them that you would like their help to post some items to your friends. Explain that they will need to help you to think about how to protect the objects so that they do not get spoiled in the post.
■ Show the children your objects and let them handle them, one by one. Ask them what they

think might happen to them if they are not protected – for example, photographs might bend and a china cup might smash.
■ Choose one item at a time and ask the children to help to you select the materials that are needed to wrap them up ready to post.
■ Focus on just two objects with younger children and present them with the materials to use. Let them touch the packaging and help them to understand how it prevents the objects from becoming damaged.
■ Encourage older children to attempt to wrap the parcels themselves.

Home links
Ask parents and carers to bring in any unwanted envelopes and packaging for the children to use in their imaginative play.

Other curriculum areas
PD Use construction materials such as LEGO to make some boxes to put precious objects in.
CD Design some pretty wrapping paper using paints.
CLL Invite the children to help you to set up your role-play area as a post office.

More ideas
■ Make protective packaging for some of the resources in your room.
■ Bring in some examples of post that you have received, and look together at the way it was packaged.

Little shoppers

What to do

■ Invite the children to help you to set up the role-play area as a food shop. Include a till, some empty shelves and surfaces to fill, and provide a large selection of 'food' for the children to explore and sort.

■ Begin by letting the children explore the food packaging. Encourage them to describe what they are doing. Ask them to think about the purpose of the packaging. For example, could they put baked beans in a mesh bag or paper packet? Why not?

■ Now ask the children to sort the shopping into different

groups, based on the type of packaging. Encourage them to stack the shelves and display the goods in their groups.

■ Invite the children to use the shop for role-play.

■ Limit the number of items for younger children to sort, and choose simple criteria such as boxes and tins.

■ Assign older children the roles of customers, shopkeepers and shelf stackers, encouraging them to swap roles at regular intervals.

More ideas

■ Provide the children with a typical selection of shopping, including some heavy and some soft or squashy objects. Ask them to pack the shopping into some small boxes, taking care not to squash or damage anything. Where will they put the heavy things?

■ Make a display of some of the shopping items, labelled with the descriptive words that the children used.

■ Visit a local shop (see the activity 'At the supermarket' on page 40) and encourage the children to notice how the food is displayed and stored.

Other curriculum areas

CD Design some attractive packaging for some supermarket items using paints or collage materials.

MD Practise counting skills in the context of the role-play environment, for example, counting out six apples into a bag.

CLL Encourage the children to discuss and plan a different type of shop for the role-play area, such as a toyshop.

Stepping Stone
Explore objects.

Early Learning Goal
Look closely at similarities, differences, patterns and change.

Group size
Up to four children.

What you need
A role-play area; selection of clean and safe shopping, and empty packaging, including cartons, tins, plastic bottles, boxes and packets; play till; paper; pens; empty shelves or surfaces.

Home links
Suggest that parents and carers let their children sort the shopping into categories, such as boxes, tins and bottles, on their next visit to the supermarket.

Colourful animals

Stepping Stone
Notice and comment on patterns.

Early Learning Goal
Look closely at similarities, differences, patterns and change.

Group size
Two to four children.

What you need
The photocopiable sheet 'Animal patterns' on page 84; the book *Roar!* by David Wojtowycz (David and Charles Children's Books); information books with pictures of a range of patterned animals; card; scissors; ribbons; colouring materials; sticky tape; sheets of blue and green paper.

What to do
■ Show the children the book *Roar!* and talk about the different animals. What patterns did they notice? (For example, the stripes of the tiger.)
■ Look at some more pictures of animals together. Ask the children to talk about the patterns on the animals' skin or fur.
■ Now explain to the children that you would like them to make their own animal-patterns book.
■ Give each child a copy of the photocopiable sheet and ask them to cut out the animals and colour them in. Show them how to stick a length of ribbon to each animal picture.
■ Encourage the children to add some details to the blue piece of paper to make it look like the sea, and some details to the green piece of paper to make it look like grassland. Cut a slit in each piece of paper so that the cut-out animals will fit into them.
■ Make a card cover for the book and attach the two animals (by their ribbons) to the inside back cover with sticky tape. Staple the two coloured pages to the book. The children will now be able to move the ribboned animals gently into the slits made in their 'environments'.
■ Instead of making a book with younger children, simply help them to make an interactive picture using one of the cut-out animals on a ribbon.
■ Encourage older children to make some extra pages with your help.

More ideas
■ Look at the way some animals use their patterns to camouflage themselves in their natural environment.
■ Let the children use model patterned plastic animals for imaginative play.

Home links
Hold a 'Pattern day' and ask parents and carers to send their children to your setting wearing something patterned.

Other curriculum areas
CD	Paint a parade of patterned animals for a wall display.
PSED	Work together to create a group animal-patterns book.

Kitchen capers

What to do

■ Ask the children about their kitchens at home. Do they help with any of the tasks in the kitchen? What equipment do they use? What equipment do the adults in their houses use?

■ With the children's help, set up the role-play area as a kitchen. Provide as much safe real kitchen equipment as possible and supplement this with play kitchen equipment.

■ Allow the children to play freely in pairs in the kitchen. Watch what they do and how they interact with the equipment.

■ Now work alongside the children and encourage them to find out how to use the

different pieces of equipment. Ask questions to encourage their thinking, for example, 'What does a sieve do?', 'How is it made?', 'Why does it need lots of tiny holes?', 'What happens when you put some bread in a toaster?', 'What do you think makes it go brown?' and so on.

■ Allow younger children to play freely with the equipment, and enhance their play by showing them how to use the different tools and pieces of equipment.

■ Invite older children to choose a piece of equipment and demonstrate its use to the rest of the group at circle time.

More ideas

■ Let the children use some of the kitchen tools to model and make marks in Plasticine.

■ Talk about other pieces of equipment that are found in the home, such as televisions, lights, lawnmowers and so on. Stress how most of them are for use only by adults.

Other curriculum areas

 PSED Talk about safety in the kitchen and alert the children to all the possible dangers.

 CD Dip some of the kitchen tools in paint and make some unusual printed pictures.

Stepping Stone
Show an interest in why things happen and how things work.

Early Learning Goal
Ask questions about why things happen and how things work.

Group size
Pairs of children.

What you need
A role-play area; play and real, safe kitchen equipment, such as a toy cooker, microwave, kettle and toaster, pots and pans, sieve, spoons, potato masher, whisk and so on.

Home links
Encourage parents and carers to let their children help them in safe and simple ways in the kitchen.

Bath toys!

Stepping Stone
Talk about what is seen and what is happening.

Early Learning Goal
Ask questions about why things happen and how things work.

Group size
Whole group, then pairs of children.

What you need
A selection of children's bath toys; water tray or baby bath; large box.

Home links
Ask parents and carers to let their children try out some floating and sinking investigations in the bath at home!

What to do
■ Invite the children to each bring in one of their favourite bath toys (with their parents' permission). Explain that you will be testing them out in the water tray. Have some other toys to hand in case of a poor response.
■ Hold a sharing time when the children bring in their toys, and let each child show their toy to the rest of the group. Ask them to explain how their toy works.
■ Put all the toys into a large box and work with pairs of children at a time. Let the children explore the toys out of the water first. Encourage them to carefully find out how they work, what each toy is made of and so on.
■ Now ask the children select a few toys to try out, one by one, in the water. Encourage them to comment on how well the toy works, what it does and so on.
■ Let younger children, in pairs, play freely, but carefully, with the toys in the water. Encourage them to talk about what the toys are doing and how they are making them do it!
■ Ask older children to sort the toys into different groups – those that float, those that wind up and so on.

More ideas
■ Make some bath toys, such as boats, from Balsa wood or silver foil.
■ Ask the children to think about their favourite toys. Which ones would be spoiled if they took them into the bath, and why?
■ Try out some other plastic, waterproof objects in the water tray, such as Sticklebricks, LEGO and plastic shapes. Do any of them float?

Other curriculum areas
CLL Read the story *Mr Archimedes' Bath* by Pamela Allen (Puffin Books) to the children.
MD Guess and count how many pebbles it takes to sink plastic boats of different sizes.

The activities in this chapter will help the children to develop a broad range of designing and making skills. The lively ideas will provide plenty of scope for working with a variety of materials while employing a wide range of techniques.

Copy cats!

What to do
■ Sit at a table with the children and make sure that each child has plenty of space in front of them. Give each child eight identical pieces of LEGO and let them play freely with them for a while.

■ Now explain that you would like each child in turn to build a shape with some (or all) of their LEGO pieces. Ask them to describe what they are doing as they work. What have they made?

■ Now ask the other children in the group to copy what the first child has done. Provide plenty of support and encouragement, and invite the first child to remind the others how they made their original model.

■ Repeat the process with each of the other children in the group.

■ Work with pairs of younger children and limit the number of pieces to four. Encourage them to wait patiently and to take turns.

■ Provide older children with pictures and simple diagrams of models and ask them to try to copy them.

More ideas
■ Repeat the process with different types of construction materials.

■ Take photographs of the models that the children make and put them in a box. Encourage the children to refer to and copy the models at a later date.

Other curriculum areas
CLL   Invite pairs of children to draw shapes and patterns for each other to copy.

MD   Develop the children's counting skills by asking them to build towers using a specified number of pieces of a construction toy.

Knowledge and understanding of the world

Goals for the **Foundation Stage**

Stepping Stone
Investigate construction materials.

Early Learning Goal
Build and construct with a wide range of objects, selecting appropriate resources, and adapting their work where necessary.

■

Group size
Two to four children.

■

What you need
Construction pieces, such as LEGO, to provide a set of eight identical pieces for each child.

Home links
Suggest that parents and carers play this 'Copy cat' game with their children at home.

Cosy cottage

Stepping Stone
Construct with a purpose in mind, using a variety of resources.

Early Learning Goal
Build and construct with a wide range of objects, selecting appropriate resources, and adapting their work where necessary.

Group size
Up to four children.

What you need
A doll's house; set of doll's house furniture; recyclable materials; fabric scraps; cotton wool; scissors; glue; sticky tape; paper; 'Snow White and the Seven Dwarfs' (Traditional).

What to do

■ Tell the children the story of 'Snow White and the Seven Dwarfs'.
■ Talk about the part of the story where Snow White tidies up the dwarfs' cottage and makes it more homely for them.
■ Show the children the doll's house and the furniture, and ask them for suggestions of ways to make it more cosy for the dolls. Add your own suggestions if they do not come up with many ideas, such as making a new sofa, some cushions for the chairs, a quilt for the bed, and so on.
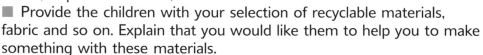
■ Provide the children with your selection of recyclable materials, fabric and so on. Explain that you would like them to help you to make something with these materials.
■ Once the children have decided what they would like to create, help them to make it, asking them for suggestions as to what materials would be best to use.
■ Keep the task simple for younger children by asking them to cut out some pieces of fabric (using safety scissors) to make some new bed covers for the dolls.
■ Let older children make several items to go into the doll's house, and encourage them to plan what they will make before they begin.

More ideas
■ Make some cushions to create a more cosy environment for your group. Put them in the story or listening corner.
■ Ask the children for other ideas of things that could be made to improve the group's environment, such as pencil pots, a newly decorated notice-board and so on.

Home links
Ask parents and carers to send their children in with some recyclable materials to replenish your stocks.

Other curriculum areas
CLL	Read other stories about houses, such as the story on the photocopiable sheet 'The Three Little Pigs' on page 85.
MD	Sort the recyclable materials by their shapes, such as round, straight and curvy, or cylinder, cube and cuboid.

Huff and puff!

What to do
■ Read the story of The Three Little Pigs to the children.
■ Remind them of the different types of materials that the pigs used to build their houses. Which material was the strongest? Why?

■ Now ask the children to consider what type of construction kit they would use to build a house that the wolf would not be able to 'huff and puff' to blow down. Let them select the kit of their choice.
■ Ask the children to each build a strong house with their chosen material. Show them how to make the joints stronger by overlapping the bricks to join the corners.
■ When the children have finished their houses, ask them to try to blow their houses over! Can they do it?
■ Choose the construction toy for younger children and help them to make a house shape, if necessary.
■ Suggest that older children make two different houses. Which one do they think is the strongest and why?

More ideas
■ Make houses out of reclaimed materials.
■ Look at some samples of sticks, straw and bricks. Compare the different textures and ask the children to think about why the sticks and the straw were not as strong as the bricks. What happens when they try to blow each thing?

Other curriculum areas
CLL · Encourage the children to retell the story as they try out their house models.
PD · Make some large-scale houses from cartons, cardboard boxes and so on.

Knowledge and understanding of the world

The inventors

Stepping Stone
Construct with a purpose in mind, using a variety of resources.

Early Learning Goal
Build and construct with a wide range of objects, selecting appropriate resources, and adapting their work where necessary.
■
Group size
Up to four children.
■
What you need
A large table; wide selection of recyclable materials; scissors; sticky tape; glue; paper; card; fabric; string.

What to do

■ Tell the children that you have filled a table with materials for them to use to make an invention. Ensure that they understand what the word 'invention' means.

■ Explain to them that a lot of the things that we have in our homes, such as televisions and washing machines, were once just ideas that people had.

■ Choose a theme, such as cleaning or kitchen equipment, and ask the children to make something that will help make things easier, for example, a machine that tidies bedrooms, or a machine that can clean an oven!

■ Help the children to think of an idea, then allow them to explore the materials to help them to decide what they will use to make it.

■ Support the children as they make their inventions, providing suggestions for fixing things or for altering their designs.

■ Let younger children simply experiment with joining materials together. Help them to think of a purpose for their masterpiece as they work (or even once it is complete!).

■ Encourage older children to formulate a plan before they begin. Help them to improve their designs as they work.

More ideas

■ Let the children decorate their finished models with paints or colouring or collage materials.

■ Find out about some inventions from the last 100 years and talk about them with the children. Use books such as *How Things Work* by Neil Ardley (Dorling Kindersley) to provide background information.

Home links
Ask parents and carers to talk to their children about the inventions that they find most useful in the home.

Other curriculum areas

PSED	Decide on a useful invention for the group and work as a team to complete it.
CLL	Write labels describing the children's inventions and display them on an interest table.

Knowledge and understanding of the world

Staircases

What to do

■ Tell the children that you are going to ask them to find out the best way of making a staircase using construction materials. Explain that you would like them to try out a few ideas using different types of bricks and construction materials.

■ Let the children play freely with the construction sets, trying out the different bricks. Show them how to make a simple staircase structure, if necessary.

■ Compare all the children's staircase models. Which bricks make the strongest staircase? What techniques have any of the children used to make the staircases stronger?

■ Encourage the children to make some more staircases, using any ideas that they gained from the first set that they made.

■ Now ask the children to consider using an inappropriate construction set to make a staircase. Can they do it? Why is it difficult?

■ Let younger children focus on one type of construction materials, and show them how to build a strong staircase with it.

■ Encourage older children to make at least three different staircases. Ask them to compare them. Which one was the easiest to make? Which one is the strongest?

More ideas

■ Fold some paper concertina-style to create a staircase effect.

■ Look at any steps or staircases in your setting. What are they made from? What other staircases do the children use (such as escalators, staircases at home, on the bus and so on)?

Other curriculum areas

CD   Dip LEGO bricks into paint and print them in a staircase pattern on a piece of paper.

MD   Count the number of bricks used to make each staircase model.

Home links
Invite any parents and carers that are builders to come in and talk to the group in simple terms about the work that they do.

Let's make a book!

Stepping Stone
Use simple tools and techniques competently and appropriately.

Early Learning Goal
Select the tools and techniques they need to shape, assemble and join materials they are using.

■

Group size
Small groups.

■

What you need
The photocopiable sheet 'Shape book' on page 86; sugar paper; scissors; pencils; colouring materials.

What to do
■ Enlarge the photocopiable sheet to A3 size and cut out the template for a shape book. Fold the pages along the dotted lines.
■ Show the children the shape book that you have created and ask them to help you to make up a simple story to fill the pages. Explain that they may use the shapes of the pages to give them ideas, for example, 'The princess ran past the trees, into the castle, up the stairs and opened the door'.

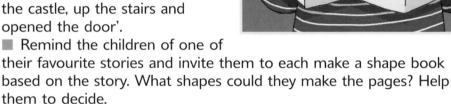

■ Remind the children of one of their favourite stories and invite them to each make a shape book based on the story. What shapes could they make the pages? Help them to decide.
■ Give each child a length of sugar paper and help them to fold it into three or four parts. Show them how to draw a shape on to the first piece, then help them as much as necessary to draw shapes on to the other parts.
■ Assist the children with cutting out the shapes that they have drawn. Encourage them to add illustrations and any writing that they are able to do, to tell the story.
■ Provide each of the younger children with a copy of the photocopiable sheet and help them to cut out the shape. Show them how to fold the page and scribe the words of their 'story' for them.
■ Encourage older children to do as much of the activity as possible independently.

More ideas
■ Use cutting and sticking techniques to make some lift-the-flap pictures and stories.
■ Make a collection of 'novelty' books for your story corner and look at the way they have been made.

Home links
Let the children take home their shape books and encourage them to explain to their parents and carers how they made them.

Other curriculum areas
CLL Make recordings of the children retelling their favourite tales. Put the tapes in your listening area and display the shape books alongside them.
CD Use felt and fabric to make some finger puppets and use them with the children's favourite stories.

Knowledge and understanding of the world

Caterpillar treats

What to do
■ Read *The Very Hungry Caterpillar* to the children. Can they remember all the food that the caterpillar ate? Look back through the story to remember all the things.
■ Now provide each child with some Plasticine or play dough and a selection of tools. Ask them to choose one of the things that the caterpillar ate and then to try to make it with their dough.
■ Show them how to use the tools to cut, shape and decorate their food. Talk about how the tools can change the shape and appearance of the things that they are making.
■ Encourage the children to share their discoveries, for example, say 'How did you make the holes in your lump of cheese, Joseph?' or 'How did you cut that slice of cake, Eleanor?'.
■ Let younger children make some food of their own choice.
■ Suggest that older children use at least three of the tools to complete their work.

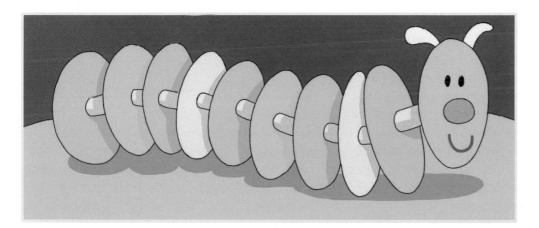

More ideas
■ Show the children how to design and make wiggly caterpillars by threading pasta tubes between coloured discs of card, adding a card disc with a face and antennae at the end.
■ Learn about the caterpillar and butterfly life cycle.
■ Hold a dolls' tea party and provide a Plasticine or play-dough feast!

Other curriculum areas
MD Make some Plasticine food to share out between a group of four toys. Make sure that each toy has the same amount.
CLL Help the children to make small books showing their own version of the story. They may, for example, choose different food for the caterpillar to eat, and he changes into something completely different!

Stepping Stone
Realise tools can be used for a purpose.

Early Learning Goal
Select the tools and techniques they need to shape, assemble and join materials they are using.
■
Group size
Up to six children.
■
What you need
The Very Hungry Caterpillar by Eric Carle (Puffin Books); Plasticine or play dough; tools to shape the Plasticine or play dough, such as spatulas, blunt plastic knives and so on.

Home links
Encourage parents and carers to let their children watch as they cook and prepare food at home. Suggest that they let their children use some of the safe equipment to help make a meal, such as whisking an egg for an omelette.

A new toy

Early Learning Goal
Select the tools and techniques they need to shape, assemble and join materials they are using.

■

Group size
Up to four children.

■

What you need
The photocopiable sheet 'Make Teddy dance' on page 87; scissors; colouring materials; split-pin fasteners; selection of soft toys and dolls that have joints and movable limbs.

Home links
Ask parents and carers to help their children to find some jointed mechanisms, such as hinges on cupboards and doors, around the home.

What to do
■ Ask the children to move their arms and legs, bending at the knees and elbows. Explain that we have special bones in our bodies, that allow us to move and bend.

■ Now look at your selection of toys with the children. Draw their attention to the way that the toys' arms and legs can be moved. Ask them to look closely at how the toys have been made.

■ Give each child a copy of the photocopiable sheet and explain that you would like them to make their own movable toy. Ask them to colour in the teddy parts and then to carefully cut them all out.

■ Demonstrate how to use the split-pin fasteners to join the teddy's arms and legs to his body. Provide support for any children who require it.

■ Invite younger children to colour in the teddy parts, but cut them out and assemble the teddy for them if necessary. Encourage them to move the teddy's arms and legs by themselves.

■ Challenge older children to complete the task as independently as possible, and praise them for their careful and accurate cutting skills.

More ideas
■ Attach the teddy to a piece of dowelling rod to make an effective stick puppet.

■ Let the children practise making jointed mechanisms with a construction set such as Meccano.

Other curriculum areas
CLL Encourage the children to bring in a toy of their own that has joints or movable parts. Ask them to tell the rest of the group about it.

PD Practise moving in a jerky manner during movement sessions.

Scrapbooks

What to do

■ Show the children your selection of notebooks. Pass these around the group and talk about the way that they are made.

■ Explain that you are going to help them to each make their own scrapbook.

■ Provide each child with some pieces of sugar paper. Show them how to fold them in half and insert them inside each other to form the pages of their scrapbooks.

■ Next, give each child a large piece of card to fold in

half to make the cover of their book. Show them how to place the pages inside the cover.

■ Now open out the pages and pierce some holes along the spine of the book with a needle. Ensure that the holes go through both the cover and the pages.

■ Thread a needle for each child and show them how to make a knot in the thread. Then demonstrate how to sew the pages to the cover using the pre-marked holes. Help the children to tie off the thread.

■ Now tell the children that you would like them to decorate their covers. Select a technique, such as marbling, weaving or collage, that the children have tried before. Help them to plan and then create their designs on a separate piece of paper.

■ Let the children stick their finished pictures to the front covers.

■ Sew the books together for younger children and let them concentrate on their cover designs.

■ For older children, mark the places for them to sew with a pencil and encourage them to carefully pierce their own holes as they sew.

More ideas

■ Make a display of handcrafted books and cards, and talk about the different techniques with the children.

■ Sew some simple cushions or beanbags for your room.

Other curriculum areas

CLL Use the scrapbooks for some drawing and writing activities.

PSED Let the children fill their scrapbooks with information about their family and friends.

At the office

Stepping Stone
Begin to try out a range of tools and techniques safely.

Early Learning Goal
Select the tools and techniques they need to shape, assemble and join materials they are using.

Group size
Whole group, then small groups.

What you need
A role-play area with a notice-board, word processor or typewriter, telephone, office stationery and so on; clay, play dough or Plasticine; reclaimed materials; glue; sticky tape; card; scissors; colouring materials.

Home links
Ask if any parents or carers who work in an office would be prepared to come in and talk to the children about their work.

What to do
■ Encourage the children to tell you if any of them have parents or carers who work in an office. Then ask them if they have ever visited an office. What does it look like?
■ Explain to the children that, with their help, you would like to turn the role-play area into an office. Set up a desk area, with a notice-board, office stationery, word processor, telephone and so on.
■ Now tell the children that

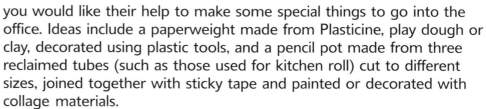

you would like their help to make some special things to go into the office. Ideas include a paperweight made from Plasticine, play dough or clay, decorated using plastic tools, and a pencil pot made from three reclaimed tubes (such as those used for kitchen roll) cut to different sizes, joined together with sticky tape and painted or decorated with collage materials.
■ Choose one of these ideas and work with the children to make their piece of office equipment.
■ Make a simple paperweight with younger children. Show them an example of a real paperweight and help them to think of ideas for decorating theirs.
■ Suggest that older children make two things for the office, and ensure that they use a range of techniques in their work.

More ideas
■ Help the children to make their own desk calendars by folding a piece of card into three to make a triangular shape, then sticking a sheet of dates or mini calendar (available from general stationers) on to one side, and photographs or pictures on to the other visible side.
■ Make some 'in-trays' from reclaimed boxes, cut to shape and covered with wrapping paper.

Other curriculum areas
CLL	Ask the children to write some memos and messages to go on the notice-board.
MD	Use some office equipment, such as paper clips, pens and so on, for counting and sorting work.

The fact that information and communication technology is all around us is reflected in the range of fun activities presented in this chapter, from observing ICT equipment in the local supermarket to developing an interactive listening area in your setting.

ICT monitor

What to do
■ Draw the children's attention to the ICT equipment that you have in your room. Explain that it is special equipment that needs to be handled and looked after carefully.
■ Tell the children that you need some help to make sure that it is used properly, and explain that each day you will choose a helper who will be called the 'ICT monitor' (or whatever name you want).
■ Explain that the monitor will be in charge of turning the television on and off, stopping and starting the tapes for any music or dance work, and they will be on hand to help the children with their computer work.
■ Think of as many ICT-related tasks as possible for the monitor to do each day. Always make sure that the tasks that you ask them to do are safe and under supervision where necessary, and ensure that the children are aware of the dangers of playing with electricity.
■ Let younger children take charge of simple tasks such as pressing a button on a remote control to activate the television or making sure that the computer table is tidy and telling an adult if the printer needs more paper or ink.
■ Show older children a new program on the computer and encourage them to show another child what to do.

More ideas
■ Write some rules with the children to explain how to look after the ICT equipment.
■ Train some of the older children in your group to teach some basic computer functions to younger members.

Other curriculum areas
CD Let the children design some colourful posters that will remind them to use the equipment carefully.
CLL Ask the children to each write down their name on a piece of paper next to the computer when they have used it, or when they have had a turn to use a new program.

Knowledge and understanding of the world

Goals for the **Foundation Stage**

Stepping Stone
Show an interest in ICT.

Early Learning Goal
Find out about and identify the uses of everyday technology and use information and communication technology and programmable toys to support their learning.

Group size
Whole group, then individuals.

What you need
A tape recorder; television; computer.

Home links
Let the ICT monitor wear a special badge or sticker home at the end of the day or session. Encourage their parents or carers to ask them what they have been doing.

At the supermarket

Stepping Stone
Show an interest in ICT.

Early Learning Goal
Find out about and identify the uses of everyday technology and use information and communication technology and programmable toys to support their learning.

Group size
Whole group.

What you need
Sufficient adult helpers to take the whole group on an outing (check Local Authority guidelines); willing supermarket or local shop.

Preparation
Arrange with your local shop or supermarket to make a visit with the children. Ask for your adult helpers to be available on that day, and send out a letter to the children's parents and carers requesting permission to take them out.

What to do
■ On the day, explain to your helpers that you would like the children to pay particular attention to the technological equipment that they will see at the supermarket or shop. These might include automatic doors, tills, bar-code scanners and intercom systems.
■ Try to arrange for the group to be shown some of these systems in operation (arrange to visit at a quiet time).
■ Divide the group into smaller groups, with an

adult helper each, and give each group a task to complete. For example, you might suggest that they buy something different towards snack time.
■ Make sure that the children pay attention to the way the food is scanned and then registered on the till. Let them see the receipt being printed and show it to them afterwards.
■ Provide close supervision for younger children, explaining what they are looking at.
■ Invite older children to use the word processor to write out a shopping list prior to the visit.

More ideas
■ Set up your role-play area as a shop and provide equipment such as a play till and calculator.
■ Invite a parent or carer who works in a shop to come in and talk to the children, in simple terms, about their job.

Home links
Tell parents and carers about the purpose of your trip and encourage them to look out for the uses of everyday technology with their children on their next visit to a supermarket.

Other curriculum areas
CLL Invite the children to try writing a shopping list to take to the shops or supermarket.

MD Fill a shopping bag with several items of shopping and ask the children to guess, and then count, the number of things that the bag contains.

The post office

What to do
■ Find out what the children know about post offices. Have any of them been inside a post office recently? What did they do there? What equipment did they see?
■ Explain to the children that you would like their help to set up the role-play area as a post office. Try to include as many pieces of ICT equipment as possible.

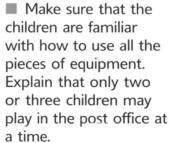

■ Make sure that the children are familiar with how to use all the pieces of equipment. Explain that only two or three children may play in the post office at a time.
■ Set up some scenarios for the children to act out, such as posting a parcel, buying some stamps and so on. Ensure that the children take it in turns to be the customer and the post-office assistant.
■ Let younger children play freely in pairs in the post office. Show them how to use some of the simple equipment, making sure that they know how to turn the objects on and off.
■ With older children, join the role-play and present them with challenges, such as asking them to weigh a parcel for you, or to print a letter from the computer.

More ideas
■ Arrange a visit to the local post office to see the equipment in action!
■ Provide some pretend (or out-of-date) forms and other stationery for the children to use in the post office.

Other curriculum areas
CD | Design some imaginative and colourful stamps to use in the post office.
MD | Do some simple weighing and comparing activities using the post-office scales.

Stepping Stone
Perform simple functions on ICT apparatus.

Early Learning Goal
Find out about and identify the uses of everyday technology and use information and communication technology and programmable toys to support their learning.

Group size
Whole group, then small groups.

What you need
A role-play area; table; chairs; equipment to set up a role-play post office, such as a calculator, computer, telephone, clock, electronic scales, rubber stamps, paper, envelopes and so on.

Home links
Ask parents and carers to provide paper, old envelopes, postcards and used stamps for the children's post office.

Guess what it is!

Early Learning Goal

Find out about and identify the uses of everyday technology and use information and communication technology and programmable toys to support their learning.

Group size

Up to six children.

What you need

A tape recorder; blank tape.

Preparation

Make a recording of some everyday sounds, such as the printer being turned on, a phone ringing, a doorbell being pressed, a kettle boiling and so on. Make sure that the sounds are quite easy to recognise and ensure that you leave a few seconds blank between each sound.

What to do

■ Tell the children that you have recorded a few sounds that they might recognise. Explain that they are sounds that they hear quite often at home or at your setting.
■ Play the sounds, one at a time, and ask the children to put up their hands when they think that they know what it is.
■ Invite one of the children to guess the sound, and see if the other children in the group thought the same.
■ Listen to the sound again and see if any children change their minds. Tell them what the sound is.
■ Repeat the process with the other sounds.
■ Ask younger children to listen to just two or three clear sounds. Let them watch as you make the sound in real life for them. Focus on developing their listening skills rather than on the correct answer.
■ Invite older children to record two or three sounds of their own for you or other children in the group to guess. Help them to operate the recording equipment.

More ideas

■ Work with groups of children to record their favourite songs or stories.
■ Make up some sound stories with the children (see the activity 'Sound story' on page 43).

Home links

Ask parents and carers to play a similar game at home. If they do not have access to recording equipment, they may play the game by blindfolding their child and making a noise for them to guess.

Other curriculum areas

PD Make a sound-effects obstacle course for the children to explore. For example, they may climb a frame to ring a bell, crawl through a hoop to shake a rattle, and so on.

PSED Record and listen to some music associated with a range of cultures and beliefs, such as reggae, bhangra and African drumming music.

Sound story

What to do

■ Read the story on the photocopiable sheet to the children without any pauses for the sound effects.

■ Give each child a percussion instrument and let them, in turn, try their instrument out.

■ Read the story again and, this time, pause where a sound symbol is marked on the page. Ask each child to make a sound with their instrument, in turn. Together, choose which sound you think best suits the noise described.

■ Once you have agreed a sound for each noise in the story, ask the children to stand in a line in the order that their instruments will be used in the story.

■ Read the story through, reminding the children when to play their instruments by tapping them gently on the shoulder. To avoid confusion, ask the children to sit down once they have had their turn.

■ Practise the story with the accompanying sounds several times, then record the sound story on to a tape. Place the tape and the instruments in the listening area for the children to return to.

■ For younger children, work with smaller groups of and give each child the same instrument. Play all the other instruments yourself and prompt the children with a nod when it is their turn.

■ Encourage older children to add extra sound effects to the story.

More ideas

■ Think of one or two sound effects that the children can make with their voices to add to the story. Do the same with other familiar stories.

■ Record the noises that the children make with the individual percussion instruments. Play them back. Can the children identify the different instruments?

Other curriculum areas

PSED Encourage the children to tell a short story about something that they do every day at home. Suggest that they add one or two sound effects.

CLL Make up a group sound story about an experience that you have shared together, such as a visit.

The listening area

Stepping Stone
Perform simple functions on ICT apparatus.

Early Learning Goal
Find out about and identify the uses of everyday technology and use information and communication technology and programmable toys to support their learning.

Group size
Individuals and pairs of children.

What you need
An area designated as your group's listening area, with comfortable seating and partitioned to keep out the noise, if possible; story, rhyme and music tapes; tape recorder and headphones (two or more if available); paper; card; story props; plastic zip-up folders.

What to do

■ Draw the children's attention to the listening area and explain to them the conditions for using it, telling them, for example, how many children are allowed and at what times.

■ Try to introduce new things to the listening area on a regular basis. For example, you could include 'story bags' (a zip-up folder containing a picture book and a tape of the same story, whether commercial or home-recorded); soft-toy characters that link with the story; props or objects that feature in the story; home-made posters advertising the story of the week, and the tape recorder and the story tape pre-loaded, ready for the children to listen to.

■ Take individuals or pairs of children into the area and help them to explore the equipment and the resources. Show them any new tapes and objects, and encourage them to work independently.

■ Work on a one-to-one basis with younger children and encourage them to listen to a short story or rhyme on a tape. Show them how to make the tape play and stop.

■ Let older children use the equipment to record their own stories (or retellings of their favourite stories). Suggest that they make a poster to advertise their story.

More ideas

■ Make some finger puppets to go with the recorded stories and put them in the story bags.

■ Set up the listening area as a recording studio and spend some time demonstrating to the children how to use the equipment to record their own voices.

Home links
Let the children borrow a story tape to listen to at home with their parents and carers.

Other curriculum areas

PSED Encourage pairs of children to record a favourite song or rhyme together.

PD Ask the children to vote for their favourite song or rhyme that they have listened to. Use the chosen song to inspire a movement activity.

Information and communication technology

Technology trail

What to do

■ Explain to the children that you would like to take them on a 'technology trail' around the room. Can they guess what they might be doing?

■ Start by telling them that they must follow you closely and help you to point out any special equipment, such as the television, radio, telephone and so on. Tell them that you will be asking them to show you how these things work.

■ As you walk around the room, stop at each piece of ICT equipment and ask the children to take it in turns to do specific tasks, such as switching on a light, turning the radio on and off, pressing a doorbell and so on. Make sure that you provide support for any new tasks.

■ Keep the activity short for younger children and concentrate on two or three simple tasks. Let them repeat them once or twice to gain confidence in the skills.

■ Encourage older children to spot the equipment and tell you about it before you draw their attention to specific tasks.

Other curriculum areas

PD Develop the children's use of controlled movements by providing a remote-controlled car for them to manoeuvre.

PSED Encourage the children to identify all the electrical appliances in your room. Talk to them about the dangers of playing with electrical equipment.

More ideas

■ Ask the children to help you to write instructions for the ICT equipment in your room. Write them up in simple list form, to place next to the relevant equipment.

■ Use the photocopiable sheet 'Spot the technology' on page 89 to talk about technological equipment that the children might find in their homes.

Stepping Stone
Show an interest in ICT.

Early Learning Goal
Find out about and identify the uses of everyday technology and use information and communication technology and programmable toys to support their learning.

Group size
Two to three children.

What you need
Your usual setting, with the ICT equipment easily accessible.

Home links
Ask the children to give their parents or carers a brief guided technology trail around your room!

Helping baby

Stepping Stone
Know how to operate simple equipment.

Early Learning Goal
Find out about and identify the uses of everyday technology and use information and communication technology and programmable toys to support their learning.

Group size
Small groups.

What you need
A selection of baby and toddler toys that involve the use of technology in some way, such as having flashing lights or making sounds, having mechanisms to wind and so on; babies and toddlers (optional).

What to do
■ Present the children with the selection of baby and toddler toys. Let them explore them.
■ Explain that you would like them to choose one of the toys and find out everything that they can about it. What does it do? Can it make a sound? Are there any lights? How does it work?
■ Allow the children some time to each explore their chosen toy, then ask them to take it in turns to tell the rest of the group what they have found about it. Help them to be as descriptive as possible, and ask them questions to encourage them to describe how the toy works.

■ Repeat the process with a different toy.
■ If possible, arrange for a few younger children to make a brief visit to your group (accompanied, of course!). Encourage the children to show the babies and toddlers the different toys.
■ Demonstrate to younger children how one of the toys works. Encourage them to take it in turns to hold the same toy and copy what you did. Repeat the process with several other toys.
■ Encourage older children to repeat the activity, this time writing down any important instructions (with an adult acting as scribe if necessary).

More ideas
■ Repeat the activity with more sophisticated toys.
■ Make a display of the toys, and add labels with the children's comments and instructions on how to operate the toys.

Home links
Suggest that the children help any younger siblings to explore and find out about their toys.

Other curriculum areas
PSED Encourage the children to talk about the games and toys that they play with at home. Then invite them to talk about the people who play with them.

MD Sort the toys in different ways, for example, those that have lights, those that make sounds, and so on.

Remote control

What to do
■ Show the children the remote-control devices. Do they know what they are? What can you do with them? Are the children allowed to use them at home?

■ Pass one of the remote controls around your group and let the children look at it more closely. Point out all the different buttons and ask the children if they know what the symbols mean.

■ Talk about the different symbols, numbers and so on together. Ask individual children to show you a certain symbol, for example, 'play', 'rewind', 'BBC 1', 'mute' and so on.

■ Now set the children certain tasks, such as 'Turn on the television', 'Put the television on standby', 'Play the tape', 'Rewind the tape' and so on.

■ With younger children, concentrate on just one of the types of remote control and encourage them to perform one task accurately.

■ Suggest that older children take it in turns to be in charge of the music system during a dance activity. Tell them when to play and stop the music, using the remote control.

More ideas
■ Look at the symbols on a music system's remote control with a child. Identify them one by one and ask the child to find the corresponding manual button on the music system.

■ Look at some other remote-control devices, such as those for operating a model car or toy.

Other curriculum areas
MD Help the children to recognise and name all the numerals that they can see on the remote controls.

CLL Develop the children's handwriting and pencil control skills by asking them to copy some of their favourite symbols from the remote-control devices.

Knowledge and understanding of the world

Finding out

Stepping Stone
Complete a simple program on the computer.

Early Learning Goal
Find out about and identify the uses of everyday technology and use information and communication technology and programmable toys to support their learning.

■

Group size
Individuals.

■

What you need
A computer with a pre-loaded simple program such as a painting program; printer; paper.

What to do
■ Find out how familiar the child is with the computer. Do they have good control of the mouse? Are they confident with the keyboard?
■ Start the computer and talk through everything that you are doing, using the correct technical words and phrases. Let the child help you if they have the confidence to do so.
■ Now tell the child that you will be showing them how to

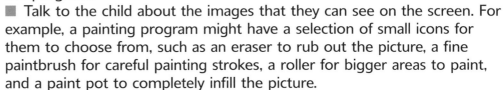

use one of the programs on the computer. Demonstrate how to 'open' the program.
■ Talk to the child about the images that they can see on the screen. For example, a painting program might have a selection of small icons for them to choose from, such as an eraser to rub out the picture, a fine paintbrush for careful painting strokes, a roller for bigger areas to paint, and a paint pot to completely infill the picture.
■ Show the child how to select the icon that they want (usually by clicking on it with a mouse) and how to select and change the colours that they would like. Help them to paint a picture of their choice.
■ Let younger children simply enjoy the painting program, with your help if necessary.
■ Encourage older children to explore several different techniques to paint different versions of the same object, for example, a house.

More ideas
■ Draw copies of icons on to pieces of card and show them to the children later on. Can they tell you what each one stands for?
■ Print the children's pictures and let each child show theirs to the rest of the group at circle time.

Other curriculum areas
PD   Draw some icons to match the ones in your painting program on to big pieces of card or paper. Provide the children with paintbrushes and a bucket of water, and do some 'playground painting' with them. Present them with the different icons and encourage them to paint accordingly!

MD   Help the children to use a simple mathematical program in a similar way.

The activities in this chapter will help the children to develop an appreciation of the passing of time, a concept that they may find difficult to understand. They will be encouraged to reflect upon past and present events in their own and other people's lives.

Yesterday

What to do

■ Check that the children understand the term 'yesterday'. Remind them what it means by giving them some examples of the things that you all did together 'yesterday'.

■ Encourage each child in turn to tell the rest of the group about something that they did or that happened yesterday. This can be a simple event, for example, they wore their red dress to your setting, or they had peanut butter sandwiches for tea!

■ Now ask the children to think of all the things that they did yesterday. Which thing would they like to draw a picture of?

■ Encourage each child to choose a simple event to draw. Ask them to tell you about their picture and scribe their words on to the back of the paper or on to a separate sheet.

■ Help younger children to remember something that they did at your setting yesterday.

■ Challenge older children to remember three things – one thing that they did in the morning, one thing that they did in the afternoon, and one thing that they did in the evening.

Other curriculum areas

CD Ask the children to sing some songs that they learned 'yesterday'.

PSED Encourage the children to remind each other of some of the things that they did together, for example, 'You played "I spy" with me, James'.

More ideas

■ Use a video recorder to record some of the events that happen at your setting, including everyday activities. Play back the video to the children to encourage the use of the relevant time vocabulary.

■ Extend the activity to remembering things that happened 'last week' or 'at the weekend'.

Goals for the Foundation Stage

Stepping Stone
Remember and talk about significant things that have happened to them.

Early Learning Goal
Find out about past and present events in their own lives, and in those of their families and other people they know.

Group size
Small groups.

What you need
Paper; pencils; colouring materials.

Home links
Ask parents and carers to reinforce the work at home by talking about things that they did with their children 'yesterday' or 'at the weekend'.

Knowledge and understanding of the world

Sleeping Beauty

Early Learning Goal
Find out about past and present events in their own lives, and in those of their families and other people they know.

■

Group size
Whole group.

■

What you need
An A3 copy of the photocopiable sheet 'After 100 years' on page 90; a copy of the traditional story 'Sleeping Beauty'.

What to do

■ Read the story to the children. Emphasise that Sleeping Beauty fell asleep for 100 years. Explain that 100 years is a very long time, and that we can see how long by looking at how much the trees and creepers grew all around the castle during that time.

■ Show the children the picture on the photocopiable sheet. Talk about how the vegetation became overgrown because it was left alone for so long.

■ Relate the overgrown plants and trees to the children's own experiences. Have any of them seen anyone cutting shrubs and trees in a garden? Do any of the children see someone cutting the grass at home or in a park? What would happen if the grass was left alone?

■ Younger children will find this a difficult concept to grasp. Keep relating the story to their own experiences of watching things grow and change in gardens and parks.

■ Let older children grow a fast-growing plant, such as some watercress or a sunflower. Suggest that they watch how the plant grows and changes over time.

More ideas

■ Take regular walks in a local park or in your group's outdoor area to look at how plants and trees are growing over time.

■ Use the picture on the photocopiable sheet to inspire the children to create colourful pictures for a display about Sleeping Beauty's castle and its overgrown grounds.

Home links
Encourage parents and carers to help their children to notice how objects in the natural world grow and change over time.

Other curriculum areas

CLL   Read some other traditional tales that show how things grow over time, such as 'The Enormous Turnip'.

CD   Do some movement work based on the story. Ask the children to twist and grow slowly to music, as they pretend to be the creepers growing outside the castle.

Grown-ups

What to do
- Tell the children that some grown-ups are coming to talk to them in groups about special occasions. Explain that you would like them to listen very carefully to what they are saying.
- Arrange for the adult volunteers to talk to groups of two or three children at a time. Explain to the 'speakers' that you would like them to encourage the children to listen carefully first, and then to contribute anything that they can think of from their own experience of special occasions.
- Ask the adults to show their photographs and

mementoes to the children. Encourage the children to look at them carefully. What do they show? Were the pictures taken a long time ago, or were they taken recently? How can they tell?
- Suggest that the volunteers talk to younger children about a special birthday celebration, as they will all be able to relate to this. Encourage younger children to remember their own birthdays, or a birthday party that they have been to.
- Help older children to think of some relevant questions to ask.

Other curriculum areas
MD Count out the correct number of birthday candles for children of different ages in your group.

CD Learn some songs about birthdays and special occasions, such as 'Candles on the Cake' in *This Little Puffin...* compiled by Elizabeth Matterson (Puffin Books).

More ideas
- Ask the children to bring in photographs of past special events in their own lives.
- Make a display of photographs showing special events at your setting. Ask the children to help you label them.

Home links
Encourage parents and carers to show and talk about old photographs with their children.

Stepping Stone
Show interest in the lives of people familiar to them.

Early Learning Goal
Find out about past and present events in their own lives, and in those of their families and other people they know.

Group size
Small groups.

What you need
Adult volunteers; their props (see 'Preparation' below).

Preparation
Send out a letter to parents and carers explaining that the children are learning about events that happened in the past. Invite them to come in and talk to small groups of children about a significant past event in their lives, such as a wedding, graduation, holiday or house move. Ask them to bring in some photographs and any mementoes of the event.

Knowledge and understanding of the world

Muddled up

Stepping Stone
Show interest in the lives of people familiar to them.

Early Learning Goal
Find out about past and present events in their own lives, and in those of their families and other people they know.

Group size
Up to four children at a time.

What you need
A selection of photographs of yourself, ranging from baby to adult.

What to do
■ Tell the children that you have a set of photographs for them to look at. Explain that they are all of you and that they show you at different times in your life.
■ Look at each photograph in random order and tell the children a little bit about it. What do they think the photographs show? How old do they think you are?

■ Now ask the children to help you to put the photographs in the right order, from baby to the present. Talk about their decisions and help them to reach agreement as a group before you place the photographs in a time line.
■ Provide a set of only three to four photographs for younger children, and make the order fairly obvious.
■ Encourage older children to look in more detail at the photographs. What clothes are you wearing? What other things have changed?

More ideas
■ Invite the children to draw a picture of how they imagine themselves to look when they have grown up!
■ Cut out some pictures of people from catalogues and magazines. Ask the children to put them in order of age.

Home links
Suggest that parents and carers show their children pictures of themselves from baby to adult. Encourage them to talk about how things have changed.

Other curriculum areas
PSED Encourage the children to talk about older members of their families, such as their grandparents and carers, or older aunts and uncles.

PD Do some movement relating to the theme of growing up and changing. Help the children to roll and crawl like babies, skip and run like children, walk like adults and shuffle like very old people!

Sharing time

What to do
◼ Invite the children to come and sit quietly in a circle. Show them your own special object, such as a wedding veil or a favourite childhood book.
◼ Tell them about the object and explain why it is important to you and the event it reminds you of. Ask them to think of an object or toy that is special to them and invite them to bring it to your setting the next day. (You may wish to send a note to parents and carers to explain the activity.)
◼ The next day, sit in a circle again and ask the children to place their special objects in a large box in the centre.

◼ Pull out the objects, one by one, and invite the owner to tell the rest of the group about it.
◼ Keep the activity short for younger children, as they will find it hard to concentrate for long.
◼ Encourage older children to talk about when and why they got the object, and to explain why it is important to them.

More ideas
◼ Keep a 'news' book for each child in your group. Help the children to record special events in their lives by a combination of various pictures and words.
◼ Together, remember an event that was special for the whole group. Create a display or make a group book to commemorate the occasion.

Other curriculum areas
PSED	Encourage the children to take it in turns to listen attentively while their friends talk about their special memories.
CLL	Listen to stories about special occasions and events, such as *Danny's Birthday* by Mike Dickinson (Hippo).
CD	Make and decorate treasure boxes to store the children's special souvenirs and mementoes.

Stepping Stone
Remember and talk about significant things that have happened to them.

Early Learning Goal
Find out about past and present events in their own lives, and in those of their families and other people they know.
◼

Group size
Whole group.
◼

What you need
An object that is special to you; space for the children to sit in a circle; large box; the children's own toys or artefacts.

Home links
Explain to parents and carers that their children are learning to use words to describe and think about the recent past. Encourage them to share memories and photographs of special events with their children.

Knowledge and understanding of the world

The doctor's surgery

Early Learning Goal
Find out about past and present events in their own lives, and in those of their families and other people they know.

Group size
Whole group, then small groups.

What you need
A role-play area set up as a doctor's surgery with play medical equipment; receptionist's desk; telephone; prescription pad; paper; pens.

Preparation
Tell the children that you would like their help to set the role-play area up as a doctor's surgery. Include a reception desk and waiting area, as well as the doctor's room.

What to do
■ Ask the children to tell you about any recent visits that they have had to the doctor's. How do they feel about seeing a doctor? Can they remember any other times when they have had to see a doctor?
■ Encourage the children to take it in turns to tell the rest of the group about an experience that they have had.
■ Now let the children take it in turns, in groups of up to four, to play in the doctor's surgery role-play area. Assign the children roles such as patient, doctor and receptionist, and help them to act out some simple scenarios, reminding them of the experiences that they have just told you about.

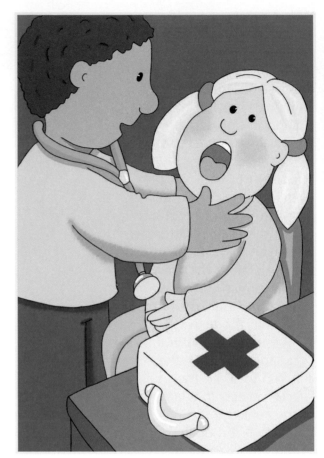

■ With younger children, go into role to keep the role-play purposeful.
■ Choose one of the children's experiences, such as a visit to the doctor's with a sore throat, and help older children to act out the sequence. Suggest that they practise it several times and then act it out in front of the rest of the group.

More ideas
■ Learn the rhyme 'Miss Polly Had a Dolly' (Traditional).
■ Send 'Get well' cards to any children in the group who have been away sick for a long period of time.

Home links
If any of the children have expressed any fears about going to the doctor's, Tell the parents or carers about it.

Other curriculum areas
| CLL | Encourage the children to write out notes, appointments and prescriptions during the course of their role-play. |
| CD | Ask the children to design and paint some healthy-living posters for the walls of the doctor's surgery. |

Achievement folders

What to do
■ Make several copies of the photocopiable sheet. Show each child their very own achievement folder and explain that each time they learn how to do something new they will be given a special certificate to put into it.
■ Let the children decorate their folders and help them to copy their names on to them if they are able.

■ Celebrate one of the children's achievements at the same time as they decorate their folder. Present them with a certificate for something that they have recently accomplished, such as learning to button their coat.
■ Let the children colour in, decorate and then place their certificates into their folders.
■ From time to time, refer to the children's folders and show them how clever they are! Talk about all the things that they can do now that they could not do before.
■ Focus on small but significant achievements with younger children, such as remembering to say 'thank you' at snack time, or sharing a toy with a friend.
■ Give older children some goals of things to achieve and encourage them to work towards these goals.

More ideas
■ Give the children stickers, as well as presenting them with a certificate, so that they can wear them on their clothes for all to see, in order to develop their confidence and self-esteem.
■ Ask the children to tell you about some of the new things that they have learned to do at home, such as riding a bicycle without stabilisers.

Other curriculum areas
 Hold a regular circle time to praise the children for all their achievements.
PD Draw the children's attention to their progress during outdoor play and movement sessions. Remind them of the things that they used to find difficult, such as climbing a frame or dribbling a ball.

Stepping Stone
Begin to differentiate between past and present.

Early Learning Goal
Find out about past and present events in their own lives, and in those of their families and other people they know.

Group size
Individuals.

What you need
The photocopiable sheet 'My certificate' on page 91; a loose-leaf folder for each child; colouring materials.

Home links
Invite parents and carers to come and see their children's work on a regular basis, and show them their achievement folders.

Knowledge and understanding of the world

Take one tree

Stepping Stone
Begin to differentiate
between past and
present.

**Early Learning
Goal**
Find out about past
and present events in
their own lives, and
in those of their
families and other
people they know.

■

Group size
Whole group.

■

What you need
A nearby tree (not
an evergreen);
camera and film;
paper; colouring
materials; extra adult
helpers (optional).

Home links
Encourage parents
and carers to discuss
the changing seasons
with their children.

What to do
■ Choose a special
tree, either in your
setting's grounds or in
the neighbourhood.
Arrange for extra
adult help if you need
to leave the premises
to go and see the
tree.
■ Explain to the
children that you are
going to 'adopt' a
tree. Tell them that
they will be finding
out all about it and
that they will look at it
regularly during the
year, to notice the
things that happen to
it and how it changes.

■ Make your first visit to the tree and take a photograph of it. Then
encourage the children to draw a picture of it. Describe the tree to them
and encourage them to look at it carefully. Does it have leaves? If so,
what shape and colour are they?

■ Repeat the activity several times during the year. Compare the
photographs of the tree and talk about how it has changed. Link the
changes to the changing seasons, to help the children to develop an
awareness of the pattern of the year.

■ With younger children, visit the tree at times of obvious change and
describe the changes in simple terms. Remind them of how the tree
looked at their last visit.

■ Invite older children to keep a record of their changing tree. Provide
each child with a small home-made
notebook and encourage them to
draw a picture of the tree in the
book each time they visit. Scribe
any words that they use to describe
the tree underneath their pictures.

Other curriculum areas
PD Make a Plasticine model
of the special tree.
MD Draw an outline of a tree
and cut out some paper
leaves. Use the leaves for
some adding and subtracting
practice, adding leaves to the
tree in spring and taking some
away in the autumn.

More ideas
■ Keep a seasonal record of the
outdoor area at your setting.
■ Display the pictures of the
changing tree and label the pictures
with the children's observations.

Knowledge and understanding of the world

When I was a baby

What to do

■ Share the story with the children. Look closely at the pictures and enjoy the surprises as you turn over the pages to discover what is behind each 'peepo' hole. Talk about how the pictures show how the baby looks at the world.

■ Use the book to begin a discussion about how the children have changed since they were babies. Look at the pictures one by one and talk about what the baby is doing, then compare with the children's experience. For example, the baby is sleeping in a cot; where do the children sleep now?

■ Now give each child a piece of paper and ask them to draw a picture of themselves as a baby (asleep in a cot, or perhaps sitting in a high chair) in the middle.

■ Next, cut out a circle from another piece of paper and place the paper over a child's picture as a peepo hole. Fix the paper down one side of the picture so that the child can pull back the peepo hole to have a look! Repeat for all the children's pictures.

■ Let younger children draw a simple picture of a baby's face, and cut out a peepo hole to fit their picture afterwards.

■ Encourage older children to write the word 'Peepo!' underneath their circle.

More ideas

■ Ask the children to draw another picture of themselves as a baby. On a separate piece of paper, ask them to draw a picture of themselves now. Stick one side of the baby picture on to the other picture to make a lift-the-flap 'then and now' picture.

■ Make a collection of stories that feature babies and toddlers, such as the *Titch* books by Pat Hutchins (Red Fox) and *When I was a Baby* by Catherine Anholt (Little Mammoth).

Other curriculum areas

MD	Keep a chart of the children's shoe measurements! Find out how their feet have grown from term to term.
CLL	Do some shared writing about the games that the children liked to play when they were babies.

Stepping Stone
Begin to differentiate between past and present.

Early Learning Goal
Find out about past and present events in their own lives, and in those of their families and other people they know.

■

Group size
Up to four children at a time.

■

What you need
The book *Peepo!* by Janet and Allan Ahlberg (Puffin Books); paper; colouring materials; scissors.

Home links
Ask parents and carers to talk to their children about how they have changed since they were babies.

Days gone by

What to do
■ Share the story with the children and enjoy the illustrations.
■ Look carefully at the illustrations again. Talk about how the pictures show how things used to be. Find some things in the pictures that have changed and talk about them with the children.
■ Start with the most obvious differences such as the old-fashioned pram and pushchair and the tin bath. Then look for some more unusual differences, for example, the old-fashioned radio and cars, the mangle and the outside toilet.
■ Encourage the children to talk about how things are different today.
■ With younger children, focus on the obvious differences in the baby equipment. Find some pictures of the modern equivalent for them to look at and compare.
■ Let older children look for some of the objects, such as radios, baths and washing machines, in a modern-day catalogue. Suggest that they cut out the pictures and compare them to the pictures in the book.

More ideas
■ Ask the children to help you to make a display of old household objects, including pictures as well as artefacts.
■ Invite the children to look at the clothes that the people in the story are wearing. Talk about how they are different from the clothes that they and their families wear today.

Other curriculum areas
PD Notice the way the children's toys are stored in a cardboard box in the story. Provide the children with reclaimed materials and invite them to make and decorate a small toy-box of their own.
MD Look closely at the illustrations in the book with the children. Help them to develop positional language by asking them to locate things on the page. For example, invite them to tell you the name of two things that can be seen under the bed, three things that are on the table, and so on.

The activities in this chapter help the children to express their likes and dislikes about the world in which they live, and encourage them to have a greater understanding of their immediate surroundings as well as places further afield.

It's a small world

What to do

■ Sit with the children at a table and show them the information books containing pictures of urban and rural environments.

■ Focus on one sort of environment at a time. For example, look at the pictures of a town and talk about everything that the children can see. Have they ever been anywhere like this? Do they live in a place like this?

■ Next, focus on the rural environments. Start by talking about what the children can see, then make some comparisons with the town that they were looking at earlier.

■ Now let the children play in pairs with some small-world play equipment. Set them the challenge of creating either a town or a country environment.

■ Work alongside the children, encouraging them to remember all the things that they saw in the pictures, as well as using their own knowledge and experience. Help them to use the relevant vocabulary to talk about what they are doing.

■ Set up a town or country environment for younger children and encourage them to use some of the correct words as they play freely with the resources.

■ Invite older children to add models made from construction materials to their environment, for example, a farm house or a hospital building.

More ideas

■ Suggest that the children draw a road layout to use with the small-world toys.

■ Play alongside the children and help them to act out scenarios in their environment, such as helping a car get through a traffic jam on its way to the hospital.

Other curriculum areas

CLL Make a word list of all the words that the children can think of associated with their environment.

PD Set out a larger version of the town environment outside, by chalking a road on to the play-area surface and using large wheeled toys.

Goals for the Foundation Stage

Stepping Stone
Show an interest in the world in which they live.

Early Learning Goal
Observe, find out about and identify features in the place they live and the natural world.

■

Group size
Up to four children at a time.

■

What you need
Information books containing pictures of towns and rural environments; small-world toys such as road maps, vehicles, houses, farms, trees and bushes.

Home links
Encourage parents and carers to help their children learn some new words to describe the area in which they live.

Where shall we live?

Stepping Stone
Show an interest in the world in which they live.

Early Learning Goal
Observe, find out about and identify features in the place they live and the natural world.

■

Group size
Up to four children at a time.

■

What you need
A playmat showing a typical town road layout, with space for adding model buildings; small-world toys.

What to do
■ Talk about the place that the children live in. What is special about it?
■ Set out the playmat and the small-world toys and explain to the children that they are going to help you to find special places for some of the small-world people to live in.
■ Provide each child in the group with some model buildings. Start by positioning the buildings, such as a hospital, some shops, a library, a church, a mosque and a school.
■ Now give each child a play person and a model house and explain, for example, that this person wants to live near to the shops, or works at the hospital and would like to live near to it.
■ Once the town has been finished and everybody is happy, let the children play freely with the resources.
■ Set up the playmat and small-world toys for younger children and talk to them about the way the town has been planned. Name the buildings and help them to use the resources for some imaginative play.
■ Encourage older children to set up the playmat for themselves. Talk to them about what they are doing and help them to consider where to place the buildings and people's houses.

More ideas
■ Provide the children with construction materials for them to make buildings to use with the playmat.
■ Take a walk in your local area to find out what amenities there are. Do people live close to many other types of buildings?

Home links
Ask carers to help their children to look at where their home is positioned. What things is it near to? What things would they like to be near to?

Other curriculum areas
CD Ask the children to paint pictures of the place that they live in.
PSED Let the children take it in turns at circle time to talk about the place in which they live.

Knowledge and understanding of the world

What's it for?

What to do

■ On the day of the walk, gather the children together and explain that you will be going for a walk in your local area to look at some 'street furniture'. Can the children guess what you mean by 'street furniture'? Explain that you mean lamp posts, signs, yellow lines, bus stops, post-boxes and so on.

■ Give your adult helpers a list of 'street furniture' to look out for.

■ Stop at each thing that you find and draw the children's attention to it. Do the children know what it is and what it is used for? Encourage them to make a guess and elaborate on their answers.

■ For younger children, draw pictures or take photographs of the objects. Show them the pictures before you go on the walk and encourage them to look out for some of the things that you showed them. Tell them a little bit about the purpose of each thing.

■ Ask older children to draw a picture of each thing. Encourage them to talk about and show their pictures back at your setting.

More ideas

■ Invite a road-safety officer to come and talk to the children.

■ Paint pictures of some of the things that the children noticed on the walk. Make a labelled display of the pictures.

Other curriculum areas

CLL Read the story *Who's Who in Our Street?* by Jan Omerod (Bodley Head) with the children.

MD Make tallies of the number of bus stops, road signs and so on that the children saw while out on their walk.

Stepping Stone
Comment and ask questions about where they live and the natural world.

Early Learning Goal
Observe, find out about and identify features in the place they live and the natural world.

■

Group size
Whole group.

What you need
Sufficient adult helpers for your group (check Local Authority guidelines); nearby urban area.

■

Preparation
Send a letter to parents and carers explaining that you will be taking the children out for a local urban walk. Invite them to volunteer to accompany you.

Home links
Encourage parents and carers to point out features of the manufactured outdoor environment to their children.

Knowledge and understanding of the world

Spotters

What to do

■ Decide what you would like the children to observe and find out about on the walk, such as doorways, walls and outside lights.

■ Give each child a clipboard, pencil and sheet of paper to take on the walk. Set out in small groups, with an adult helper for each group.

■ Give the adult helpers a list of things to look out for and explain that you would like them to draw the children's attention to any examples that they notice.

■ Encourage the children to choose one of the topics, such as outside lighting, and to draw examples of this on their sheet of paper, such as a lamppost and a security light.

■ Back at your setting, talk about all the things that you noticed. Suggest that the children share their drawings with the rest of the group at circle time.

■ With younger children, concentrate on one type of thing, such as doorways. Help them to find several examples, such as a shop doorway, a house front door and the doors to the local school.

■ Invite older children to make comparisons and express personal opinions about the things that they see. For example, they might prefer brick walls to concrete walls, or comment on the graffiti left on a wall or doorway.

More ideas

■ Prior to your walk, take photographs of features that you would like the children to spot. Divide the children into groups and give each group a photograph of a feature, asking them to look out for the object.

■ Talk to the children about why we need outside lighting.

Other curriculum areas

CD Take some crayon rubbings of interesting objects on the walk.

PD Make some clay models of features such as door numbers or door knockers.

Knowledge and understanding of the world

Town or country?

What to do
■ Tell the children the story and talk to them about the differences between the life of the Town Mouse and the life of the Country Mouse.
■ Talk about where the children live. Would they like to live somewhere else? Where would they live?
■ Put up the backing paper and draw a vertical line down the middle. Tell the children that they are going to help you to make a 'Town and country' frieze.
■ Work with small groups of children to contribute to the display. Start by sponge-painting the backing paper, to show the sky in both halves of the frieze. Sponge-paint green grass for the country side of the frieze, and ask a child to paint grey roads on to the town side.
■ Decide together what you will include on each half of the frieze.
■ Ideas for the country include a tractor made from reclaimed materials, painted and glued on to the display; some ears of wheat stuck to the backing paper; a collage picture of a farmhouse, and some patchwork fields made from fabric.
■ Ideas for the town include houses and shops made from reclaimed materials and then painted; paintings or drawings of buses and vehicles, and paintings of people.
■ Allocate simple tasks, such as the sponge-painting, to younger children.
■ Give older children more complicated challenges such as making the three-dimensional models.

More ideas
■ Place a table beneath the display and set up some small-world resources, such as farm animals, vehicles and so on.
■ Label the display with the correct geographical terms.

Stepping Stone
Show an interest in the world in which they live.

Early Learning Goal
Observe, find out about and identify features in the place they live and the natural world.
■
Group size
Whole group, then small groups.
■
What you need
The photocopiable sheet 'Tale of two mice' on page 92; backing paper in a neutral colour; sugar paper; paints; painting sponges; collage materials; glue; reclaimed materials; scissors; colouring materials; pencils.

Home links
Send home copies of the story for the children to enjoy with their parents and carers at home.

Other curriculum areas
CD — Learn some town and country songs such as 'The Wheels on the Bus' (Traditional).
PD — Use boxes and cartons to make a large vehicle to display alongside the children's work.

Knowledge and understanding of the world

Word books

What to do

■ Tell the children a story that is set in the town or countryside, for example, 'Tale of two mice'.

■ Encourage them to talk about all the words that describe one of those places, such as fields, tractor, roads, cars and so on.

■ Give each child a copy of the photocopiable sheet 'Where can you find them?' and talk about the pictures together. Which things belong in the town? Which things belong in the countryside?

■ Ask the children to cut out the pictures carefully and to colour them in. Suggest that they stick them into their home-made books. Help them to write the words underneath the pictures.

■ Cut out the pictures for younger children and let them stick them into their books in any order. Write the words for them.

■ Suggest to older children that they arrange the pictures into groups of town or country words, and that they try writing the words themselves. Encourage them to write a 't' for 'town' or a 'c' for 'country' next to each of the pictures.

More ideas

■ Ask each child to draw a town or countryside picture on to the front cover of their book, and the opposite picture on to the back cover.

■ Add extra pages to the books and either let the children draw further pictures on the pages or suggest that they find, cut and stick suitable pictures from magazines or catalogues.

Home links
Let the children take home their finished word books and encourage them to add some further pages at home with their parents' help.

Other curriculum areas

MD Sort small-world toys into sets of town and country objects.

CD Cut out one set of the pictures from the photocopiable sheet and invite the children to incorporate them into a collage picture of the town or the countryside.

Litterbugs

What to do

■ Talk to the children about litter. Do they see any outside on the streets near by? Where should people put litter?

■ Empty the contents of your waste paper bin on to a large sheet of paper and let the children look at the items. Talk about where the rubbish came from and why it is in the bin. What other things do people throw away? Do any of the children know what 'recycling' means? What things can be recycled?

■ Now tell the children that you would like them to make their own 'litterbugs'. Ask them to imagine that the litterbug is a friendly creature that goes around helping to pick up the rubbish.

■ Provide each child with a sheet of A4 paper and show them the selection of collage materials. Let them use the materials freely to create an imaginary creature.

■ For younger children, you may wish to draw an outline of a litterbug for them to decorate with the collage materials.

■ Encourage older children to make a three-dimensional litterbug using reclaimed materials.

More ideas

■ Set up a recycling point in your room and arrange for the paper and plastic to be recycled on a regular basis.

■ Take a walk in the local area and carry out a litter survey. Where do you notice litter? Where are the bins positioned?

Other curriculum areas

CLL Encourage the children to each give their litterbug a name, and invite them to tell you all about their creatures – what they like to eat, how old they are and so on.

MD Sort some 'clean' rubbish into different groups, such as paper, plastic and so on.

Stepping Stone
Comment and ask questions about where they live and the natural world.

Early Learning Goal
Find out about their environment, and talk about those features they like and dislike.
■
Group size
Up to five children at a time.
■
What you need
A waste-paper bin; 'clean' rubbish such as paper, empty drinks cartons, sweet-wrappers, pencil shavings, empty yoghurt carton, empty crisp bag and so on; collage materials such as pompoms, feathers, tissue paper, shiny paper, buttons, sequins (take care with small items for younger children); glue sticks; large sheet of paper; sheets of A4 paper scissors; colouring materials.

Home links
Encourage carers to take part in your recycling project. Ask for volunteers to take the paper to a recycling bank.

Lots of pots

What to do
■ Take the children into the outside area and ask them to take a good look around.
■ Back inside, ask the children to tell you what they noticed about the area. What did they like? What did they think looked messy?
■ Ask them to think of some ideas to make the outside area look more attractive. Help them by making some suggestions, such as providing some new plant pots and filling them with plants, storing the equipment in clean, bright boxes, sweeping up any old leaves and rubbish, and so on.
■ Explain to the children that you are going to ask them to help you to tidy up the area. Take them out in groups, with an adult helper for each group, and carry out some of your own and the children's ideas.
■ Once you have implemented all your ideas, invite the children to comment on the changes.
■ Let younger children carry out simple tasks such as sweeping up or washing outside windows.
■ Invite older children to help you to plant some seeds or bedding plants in the containers.

More ideas
■ Ask your premises officer if you can paint some new playground patterns on to the outside area.
■ Have a sort-out of all your outside play equipment. Involve the children in arranging the equipment in different sets.

Other curriculum areas
CLL Let the children chalk some words and pictures on the ground to decorate it (provided that they help you to wash them off later!).
PSED Agree on some rules for sensible outdoor play with the children.

Favourite places

What to do
■ The day before the activity, explain to the children that you will be talking about their favourite outdoor places. Ask them to remember to bring in a postcard or photograph that shows somewhere they have been or like going to. You may wish to send a note home to parents and carers, or put up a notice in your window.

■ The next day, gather the children together in your carpet or quiet area and remind them that you will be thinking about outdoor places.

■ Start by asking the children what their favourite places are. Make a list of them on an easel or board.

■ Next, invite the children to take it in turns to show their picture (if they have one) and to tell the rest of the group about a time that they went to this place.

■ Encourage each child to try to describe the place. Help them to do this by asking them questions such as, 'Is it a busy place?', 'What can you do there?' and so on.

■ With younger children, work with smaller groups of three or four children, as their concentration span will be more limited.

■ Suggest that older children tell you about two different places that they like going to. Ask them to tell you what is different about each one.

More ideas
■ Let the children bring in some holiday souvenirs to show to the rest of the group. Encourage them to ask each other questions about their trips.

■ Make a table-top display of pictures and souvenirs from days out, favourite places and holidays.

Stepping Stone
Show an interest in the world in which they live.

Early Learning Goal
Find out about their environment, and talk about those features they like and dislike.
■
Group size
Whole group.
■
What you need
The children's own photographs and postcards; board or easel; pen.

Other curriculum areas
PSED Encourage those children that worship regularly to tell the rest of the group about the special indoor place that they visit, such as the church, mosque and so on.

CD Invite the children to draw or paint pictures of their favourite outdoor places.

Home links
Invite parents and carers to accompany the group on a pleasure outing to a nearby park for a picnic.

Knowledge and understanding of the world

All kinds of homes

What to do

■ Explain to the children that you are going to help them to find out about a variety of different types of homes.

■ Ask the children to tell you a little bit about the type of home that they live in. Is it a house? A flat? A caravan?

■ Enlarge a copy of the photocopiable sheet and look at the different types of homes. Talk about them together.

■ Now share a book that also shows lots of different types of

homes. Invite the children to talk about what they like and dislike about each one. Where would they like to live?

■ Now ask the children to choose one of the types of homes. Present them with the reclaimed materials and resources, and help each child to plan and make a model of their choice.

■ Provide a simple house-shaped box for younger children. Suggest that they paint it, then help them to cut out and stick on pieces of card as doors and windows.

■ Encourage older children to plan what they will make, selecting the resources and then implementing their designs.

More ideas

■ Paint some pictures of the homes before you make the models.

■ Make a bar chart showing the types of homes that the children and adult helpers live in. Which is the most popular?

Other curriculum areas

CD Ask each child to paint or draw an imaginative picture of their house of the future.

CLL Fold a piece of sugar paper in half and cut it into a house shape. Draw on windows and a door. Give one to each child and invite them to open it and draw their own family living inside it.

Knowledge and understanding of the world

This chapter provides activities that will help the children to develop their sense of identity as well as their place, and the place of other people, within society. Ideas include tasting and preparing cultural foods, discussing personal events and listening to African music.

Special events

What to do

■ Gather the children together for circle time and tell them about an important event that has happened to you at some time in your life. Tell them how you felt on that day.

■ Explain that each day, at circle time, you will be asking two or three children to do the same.

■ Invite your first volunteers to speak. Help them to remember as much as they can about the event – it might be their first day at your setting, the birth of a sibling and so on. Ask them how they felt at the time. Were they very excited? Were they nervous?

■ After each circle time, invite the children who have spoken to each come and draw a picture to commemorate the event. They should include themselves in the picture.

■ Help the children to each cut out a simple card border to use as a frame for their picture. Cut the card so that it frames the picture, and glue it on to the paper. Add a piece of folded card as a stand-up support, attaching it with glue.

■ Talk individually to younger children about a special event and ask them to draw the event at the same time as you talk about it.

■ Make more sophisticated frames with older children. Use two pieces of card (one with a square shape cut out) and glue them together on three sides, then insert the picture inside the frame.

More ideas

■ Let the children each bring in photographs and mementoes of their special event to share with the rest of the group.

■ Make a list of all the children's special events and display the children's framed pictures next to it.

Other curriculum areas

PSED ■ Encourage the rest of the group to listen attentively to the child who is speaking.

CD ■ Invite the children to decorate their frames with collage materials such as sequins, buttons, pieces of shiny paper and so on.

Knowledge and understanding of the world

Stepping Stone
Express feelings about a significant personal event.

Early Learning Goal
Begin to know about their own cultures and beliefs and those of other people.

Group size
Whole group, then individuals.

What you need
Paper; pencils; colouring materials; thin card; scissors; glue sticks.

Home links
Invite parents and carers to come and see their children's pictures, and encourage each child to tell their carers how they described their special event.

Year scrapbook

Early Learning Goal
Begin to know about their own cultures and beliefs and those of other people.

Group size
Whole group, then small groups and individuals.

What you need
A large scrapbook; colouring and drawing materials; scissors; glue; souvenirs and photographs of group events.

What to do

■ Show the children the large scrapbook and explain that you will use this book over the course of the year to record all the important events and news of the group.

■ Invite a small group of children to help you to decorate the front cover of the book, asking them for ideas of what to call the book.

■ Over the course of the year, fill the scrapbook with photographs, souvenirs and records of the special events that take place in your setting. Make sure that all the children contribute to the book, for example, by doing some shared writing about a group outing. Ensure that each child draws at least one picture to go into the scrapbook.

■ Encourage younger children to contribute lots of visual material, such as decorative borders and drawings. They will also enjoy pasting in photographs and souvenirs under your supervision.

■ Suggest that older children help you with the writing for the scrapbook. They will enjoy using the word processor to copy up snippets of shared writing, and they can also be encouraged to help to take the photographs that will go into the book.

More ideas

■ With the children's help write a weekly report of the group's activities to include in the book.

■ At intervals throughout the year, read the book to the children and encourage them to remember the outings and events that are described.

Home links
Have a book ceremony at the end of the year. Invite parents and carers to come in and see the group scrapbook and the children's other book-making projects.

Other curriculum areas

CLL Ask the children to contribute captions for the pictures that they draw for the scrapbook.

CD Make decorative pockets to glue into the scrapbook. Use the pockets for the children's favourite pieces of artwork.

Our group

What to do
■ Share the information books about children around the world with the whole group. Talk about what the children find interesting about the other children.
■ Tell the children that you are going to help them to make a special book all about the children in the group. Explain that each page of the book will be about a different child.
■ Either take a photograph of each child, or ask the children to bring one in from home that can be included in the book.
■ Glue each child's photograph on to their own page, then ask each child to tell you a little bit about themselves, their family and the place in which they live. Write down what the children say and keep the text ready to include in the book.

■ Write down younger children's 'autobiographies' for them. Read back what they said to you.
■ Encourage older children to do some writing of their own on their pages. They may also like to copy their own 'autobiography' notes.

More ideas
■ Take a photograph of the whole group and include it at the back of the book. Write some information about the group's favourite activities.
■ Ask the children to compare the group's book with the information books that they looked at. Is there anything else that they would like to include in their book?

Other curriculum areas
PSED Encourage the children to find out about another child's favourite hobby.
MD Use the information in the group book to make some bar charts, counting the children who have brothers, blue eyes and so on.

Stepping Stone
Describe significant events for family or friends.

Early Learning Goal
Begin to know about their own cultures and beliefs and those of other people.

Group size
Whole group, then small groups.

What you need
Information books showing children around the world, such as *Children Just Like Me* by Barnabas and Anabel Kindersley (Dorling Kindersley); home-made book with a page for each child; paper; scissors; photographs of the children; writing and colouring materials.

Home links
Put the book in your group's reception area for parents and carers to look at with their children.

African experience

Early Learning Goal
Begin to know about their own cultures and beliefs and those of other people.

Group size
Small groups.

What you need
African instruments such as a thumb piano and African drums (aim for one instrument per child); CD player or tape recorder; African music such as *Master Drummers of Africa* by various artists (ARC) or *The Ultimate Collection* by Ladysmith Black Mambazo (Wrasse) (for some African vocal sounds). Alternatively, do a music search under the international category on the Internet at www.amazon.co.uk

What to do
■ Tell the children that they are about to have an African experience!
■ Play them your chosen African music and invite them to listen to it carefully. What instruments can they hear? What do they make them think of?
■ Listen to the music again and see if they notice anything new.
■ Now show the children your African instruments. Carefully pass each around the group, encouraging the children to look at how it is made and listening to any sound that it can make.
■ Next, demonstrate to the children how to play one of the instruments and pass it around again, letting each child have a turn to play it. Repeat with the other instruments.
■ Now give each child an instrument to play and let them strum or bang along as you play the music to them again!
■ Younger children will need to listen to short bursts of the music only and will need more time to play freely with the instruments.
■ Encourage older children to pick up the beat of the music and to play along accordingly.

More ideas
■ Listen to some music from other cultures, such as Indian sitar music or Greek music.
■ Put a selection of different cultural instruments on a table for the children to explore.

Home links
Invite the children to bring in some music that they enjoy listening to at home.

Other curriculum areas
CD Learn some songs from other cultures, such as 'Okki-tokki-unga' in *Okki-tokki-unga* (A & C Black), which tells of an Eskimo boy's adventures.
MD Sort a range of musical instruments by shape and size.

Food from Mexico

What to do

■ Ask parents and carers permission for the children to taste food, and check for any allergies and dietary requirements.

■ Invite the children to tell you about their favourite kinds of foods. Do they like spicy food? Junk food? Food from other countries?

■ Tell them that they are going to find out about some food from Mexico, taste some Mexican food and make some of their own.

■ Show the group the pictures of Mexican food and find out if any of the children have tried it before.

■ Follow the recipe on the photocopiable sheet to make some spicy salsa. Involve the children in mixing the ingredients and spooning the salsa into small bowls when it is ready.

■ Put out all the different Mexican treats into the medium-sized bowls and invite the children to sample the food at snack time.

■ Younger children may be more reluctant to try out the new foods. Let them start with the most bland ones first.

■ Suggest that older children write out labels for each of the foods to display in front of the bowls.

More ideas

■ Try out a different food theme every week and do some fun cookery activities together.

■ Compile an 'Around the world' recipe book from all the different recipes that you try out with the children.

Stepping Stone
Gain an awareness of the cultures and beliefs of others.

Early Learning Goal
Begin to know about their own cultures and beliefs and those of other people.

Group size
Small groups.

What you need
The photocopiable sheet 'Spicy salsa' on page 95; the ingredients listed on the sheet; large bowl; small and medium-sized bowls; chopping board; sharp knife (adult use); pictures of Mexican food, such as those found in a Mexican cookery book; tortilla chips; soft corn tortillas; guacamole; plates; bowls; spoons.

Home links
Ask parents and carers to fill in a form about their child detailing any information regarding food allergies and dietary requirements.

Other curriculum areas

CLL Read the Mexican tale of 'The Corn Maidens' in *Our Favourite Stories from Around the World* by Jamila Gavin (Dorling Kindersley) to the children.

CD Make some Mexican-style place mats, using Aztec designs, to place the food on.

Knowledge and understanding of the world

World food festival

Stepping Stone
Gain an awareness of the cultures and beliefs of others.

Early Learning Goal
Begin to know about their own cultures and beliefs and those of other people.

Group size
Whole group.

What you need
A range of foods from a variety of different cultures; bowls; dishes; spoons; paper; card; colouring and writing materials; cookery books with international recipes.

Preparation
Write to parents and carers explaining that you will be holding a 'World food festival' at your setting, where the children will have the opportunity to try a range of foods from different cultures. Ask them to tell you of any food allergies and dietary requirements that their children have.

What to do
■ Prepare the children for the day by sharing with them some cookery books that show a range of international foods. Talk to them about the kinds of foods that you will be providing and explain that they will be able to try them if they wish.
■ Get some decorations ready for your food festival, with the children's help. Ideas include brightly coloured place mats with cultural patterns, flags from different countries, and tissue-paper flower arrangements and garlands to decorate the table.
■ On the day of the festival, set up the food table with the decorations and lay out your selection of food in dishes. Let the children take a plate and sample a selection of dishes of their choice. Encourage them to describe and compare the different tastes.
■ Ask an adult to accompany younger children as they choose and taste some of the food.
■ At the end of the festival, invite older children to tell the rest of the group about the dish that they enjoyed the most. Find out how many children liked the same dish the best.

More ideas
■ Hold a multicultural parade before the festival. Invite the children to play multicultural instruments as they march around the room.
■ Make a colourful banner with the words 'World food festival' to drape across the entrance to your room.

Home links
Ask parents and carers to help with the food festival, inviting them to attend and to provide a dish from their own or another culture for the children to try.

Other curriculum areas
CLL Ask the children to copy out labels for the different foods on to pieces of card, to display next to the dishes.
MD Make repeating-pattern paper chains to decorate the food table.

Knowledge and understanding of the world

Multicultural tales

What to do
■ Select a special story from your collection each day and tell the story at a regular time, such as during circle or story time.
■ Think of some interesting activities for the children to do after they have heard the stories. For example, they could make some corn tortillas after hearing the Mexican tale of 'The Corn Maidens', or they could make model castles after hearing the story of 'Puss in Boots'.
■ Across the week, build up a portfolio of the children's artwork, story reviews and retellings.

Compile them into a decorated folder and include them as part of a display celebrating your 'Multicultural story' week.
■ Focus on two stories with younger children and base your week's work around them.
■ Provide older children with a home-made book and suggest that they write a simple review and draw a picture of each story. Make a display of the children's very own multicultural story-books at the end of the week.

More ideas
■ Make a display of stories from around the world and encourage the children to browse through them.
■ Retell one of the children's favourite stories, this time inviting them to take on the different roles and encouraging them to act out their parts as you tell the story.

Other curriculum areas
CLL Hold a 'Favourite story' week, encouraging the children to bring in their favourite books to talk about to the rest of the group.
PSED Ask the children to tell you about the stories that they hear at home. Do they have any family favourites?

Home links
Invite parents and carers to come in and tell or read the children a favourite story from their own culture (check that the stories are suitable for the age group beforehand).

Early Learning Goal
Begin to know about their own cultures and beliefs and those of other people.

Group size
Whole group.

What you need
A source of multicultural tales, such as *Our Favourite Stories from Around the World* by Jamila Gavin (Dorling Kindersley); art and craft materials; writing and colouring materials.

Preparation
Plan a week of multicultural storytelling and associated activities. Tell parents and carers about your project and encourage their involvement. If possible, arrange for a story-teller to come in and give a performance for your group.

Knowledge and understanding of the world

Raven's bag

Stepping Stone
Gain an awareness of the cultures and beliefs of others.

Early Learning Goal
Begin to know about their own cultures and beliefs and those of other people.

Group size
Whole group, then small groups.

What you need
The photocopiable sheet 'The coming of Raven' on page 96; pieces of brown fabric, big enough to fold into two to make a bag; scissors; blunt needles and thread; discs of yellow card; glue sticks; yellow, gold and orange tissue paper.

What to do
■ Tell the children the traditional Inuit tale on the photocopiable sheet. Talk about the story together.
■ Remind the children of the part in the story where the Raven stuffs the sun into the bag. Can they remember why he did this?
■ Now work with the children, in small groups, to make bags like Raven's. Fold the brown fabric in half and help each child to make stitches along each side, to create a simple bag.

■ Next, give each child a disc of card and show them how to tear up pieces of the coloured tissue paper to scrunch up and stick on to their disc to make a sun.
■ Put the finished card suns inside the bags and encourage the children to use the bags and suns to mime parts of the story, as you tell them the story again.
■ Make the bags for younger children and help them to cover their card suns with tissue paper, ready to put in their bags.
■ Make fabric handles for the bags with older children, and encourage them to retell the appropriate parts of the story with you.

More ideas
■ Use an information book to find out what a raven looks like.
■ Encourage the children to paint or draw pictures of the story. Read them the story again to give them ideas.

Home links
Let the children take home a copy of the tale, as well as their bags and suns. Encourage parents and carers to enjoy the story with their children.

Other curriculum areas
PD	Create a landscape of trees and mountains in the sand tray.
CLL	Make a collection of stories from different cultures that talk about the natural world.

Knowledge and understanding of the world

International café

What to do

■ Talk to the children about the café. Explain that it is a café that sells a range of food from different cultures and countries.

■ Ask the children to talk about the kind of food that they like to eat. What sort of food do they eat at home?

■ Talk about the kind of food that might be sold in your café, giving them ideas as necessary. Write the suggestions on to an easel that can be used as the menu board.

■ Show the children the special equipment that you have provided. Explain what it is used for and how it is used.

■ Let the children play freely, in small groups, in the café.

■ Go into role alongside younger children in the café to help them to play fairly with one another and to give them ideas for their play.

■ Assign roles to older children and encourage them to work together co-operatively.

More ideas

■ Arrange to cook some snacks each day to serve in the café at your usual snack time.

■ Put up posters and pictures showing a range of different countries and cultural traditions in your café.

Other curriculum areas

CLL Help the children to write out menus and price lists for the café.

MD Set out the tables in the café, making sure that each child and place setting have the right number of knives, forks, plates, cups and so on.

Stepping Stone
Gain an awareness of the cultures and beliefs of others.

Early Learning Goal
Begin to know about their own cultures and beliefs and those of other people.

Group size
Small groups.

What you need
A role-play area set up as a café, with tables, chairs, cloths, menus, paying point and so on; artefacts and equipment from a variety of cultures, such as Thali dishes, chopsticks, Chinese bowls and tea set, American-style take-away boxes, and so on; pretend or real food; card; paper; pens; easel.

Preparation
With the children's help, set up the role-play area as a café.

Home links
Invite parents and carers to volunteer to come in and cook some dishes with the children, to serve in the café.

Traditional dress

Stepping Stone
Gain an awareness of the cultures and beliefs of others.

Early Learning Goal
Begin to know about their own cultures and beliefs and those of other people.

Group size
Whole group.

What you need
An information book that shows examples of traditional dress around the world, such as the book *Children Just Like Me* by Barnabas and Anabel Kindersley (Dorling Kindersley); some examples of traditional dress such as a sari or shalwar kameez; the children's own special clothes (if possible).

Preparation
Send home a letter, or put up a notice, explaining that the children will be finding out about traditional dress and special clothes. Ask parents and carers if they can send their children in with some special clothes of their own, such as a bridesmaid's dress.

What to do
■ Show the children the information book and talk to them about the special clothes that the children are wearing.
■ Ask the children to tell you about any special clothes that they like to wear. Does anyone in their family wear special clothes? Do any of the children's parents or carers wear uniforms or special clothes when they go to work?
■ Share with the children the special, traditional clothes that you have brought in to show them. Tell them a little bit about when and why the clothes are worn.
■ Invite any children who have brought in special clothes to take it in turns to volunteer to show their clothes to the rest of the group.
■ With younger children, work in small groups. Let them touch and explore the clothes that you have brought in.
■ Encourage older children to listen carefully to one another as they talk about their special clothes.

More ideas
■ Think of other occasions when people wear special clothes, such as for sport or for dressing-up in plays.
■ Put some traditional clothes from other cultures in your dressing-up box.

Home links
Invite any parents or carers who wear special uniforms for their work to come in and show them to the children.

Other curriculum areas
CLL Ask the children to each draw a picture of themselves in their favourite or some special clothes. Encourage them to tell you about their drawings, and scribe some words for them underneath their pictures.

CD Look at some multicultural bead work and jewellery. Invite the children to make up some designs of their own using beads and collage materials.

Daily activity sheet

Description of activity	Group size
	Children to focus on
Learning objectives/curriculum area	

Resources	Key vocabulary/ questions	Observations/notes
Support and extension ideas		

Exploration and investigation

Name _____

Goals	Assessment	Date
Exploration and investigation		
Investigate objects and materials by using all of their senses as appropriate.		
Find out about, and identify, some features of living things, objects and events they observe.		
Look closely at similarities, differences, patterns and change.		
Ask questions about why things happen and how things work.		

Photocopiable   **Knowledge and understanding of the world**

Designing and making, ICT

Name _____

Goals	Assessment	Date
Designing and making skills		
Build and construct with a wide range of objects, selecting appropriate resources, and adapting their work where necessary.		
Select the tools and techniques they need to shape, assemble and join materials they are using.		
Information and communication technology		
Finds out about and identify the uses of everyday technology and use information and communication technology and programmable toys to support their learning.		

Time, place, cultures and beliefs

Name _____

Goals	Assessment	Date
Sense of time		
Find out about past and present events in their own lives, and in those of their family and other people they know.		
Sense of place		
Observe, find out about and identify features in the place they live and the natural world.		
Find out about their environment, and talk about those features they like and dislike.		
Cultures and beliefs		
Begin to know about their own cultures and beliefs and those of other people.		

Photocopiable **Knowledge and understanding of the world**

Making a nest box

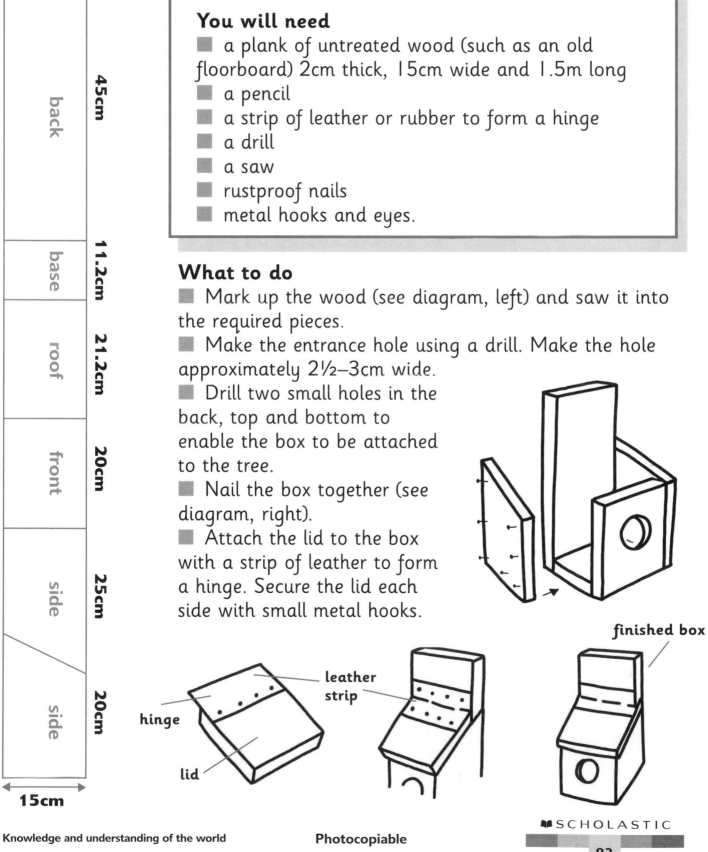

back

45cm

base

11.2cm

roof

21.2cm

front

20cm

side

25cm

side

20cm

15cm

You will need
■ a plank of untreated wood (such as an old floorboard) 2cm thick, 15cm wide and 1.5m long
■ a pencil
■ a strip of leather or rubber to form a hinge
■ a drill
■ a saw
■ rustproof nails
■ metal hooks and eyes.

What to do
■ Mark up the wood (see diagram, left) and saw it into the required pieces.
■ Make the entrance hole using a drill. Make the hole approximately 2½–3cm wide.
■ Drill two small holes in the back, top and bottom to enable the box to be attached to the tree.
■ Nail the box together (see diagram, right).
■ Attach the lid to the box with a strip of leather to form a hinge. Secure the lid each side with small metal hooks.

finished box

leather strip

hinge

lid

Knowledge and understanding of the world   **Photocopiable**

■SCHOLASTIC

Animal patterns

Cut out the animals and colour in the patterns.

Photocopiable   **Knowledge and understanding of the world**

The Three Little Pigs

Once upon a time there were three little pigs, who set off into the big, wide world.

The first little pig built a house out of straw.

The second little pig built a house out of sticks.

The third little pig built a house out of bricks. And then they settled down to live their lives.

One night, someone knocked on the door of the straw house.

'Little pig, little pig, let me in,' said the voice of the Big, Bad Wolf.

'No, no, no,' cried the first pig. 'I will not let you in – by the hairs on my chinny chin chin!'

'Then I'll huff and I'll puff and I'll blow your house down!' bellowed the wolf. And he huffed and he puffed so hard that the house of straw came tumbling down.

The first little pig rushed off to his brother's house of sticks and was saved.

The next night, someone knocked on the door of the stick house.

'Little pig, little pig, let me in,' said the voice of the Big, Bad Wolf.

'No, no, no,' cried the second pig. 'I will not let you in – by the hairs on my chinny chin chin!'

'Then I'll huff and I'll puff and I'll blow your house down!' roared the wolf. And he huffed and he puffed so hard that the house of sticks came tumbling down.

The first little pig and the second little pig rushed off to their brother's house of bricks and were saved.

The next night, someone knocked on the door of the brick house.

'Little pig, little pig, let me in,' said the voice of the Big, Bad Wolf.

'No, no, no,' cried the third pig. 'I will not let you in – by the hairs on my chinny chin chin!'

'Then I'll huff and I'll puff and I'll blow your house down!' roared the wolf. And he huffed and he puffed so hard that – *nothing happened!*

'You can't beat me!' cried the wolf, 'I'm coming down the chimney!'

Then, up on to the roof he climbed and down the chimney he went.

'Quick!' cried the pigs, and they filled up the cauldron on the fire with hot water.

Then down slid the wolf, splosh! into the cauldron of boiling water. And that was the end of him.

Which left the three little pigs living together happily ever after, in the house of bricks.

Irene Yates

Shape book

Cut out and fold along the dotted lines.

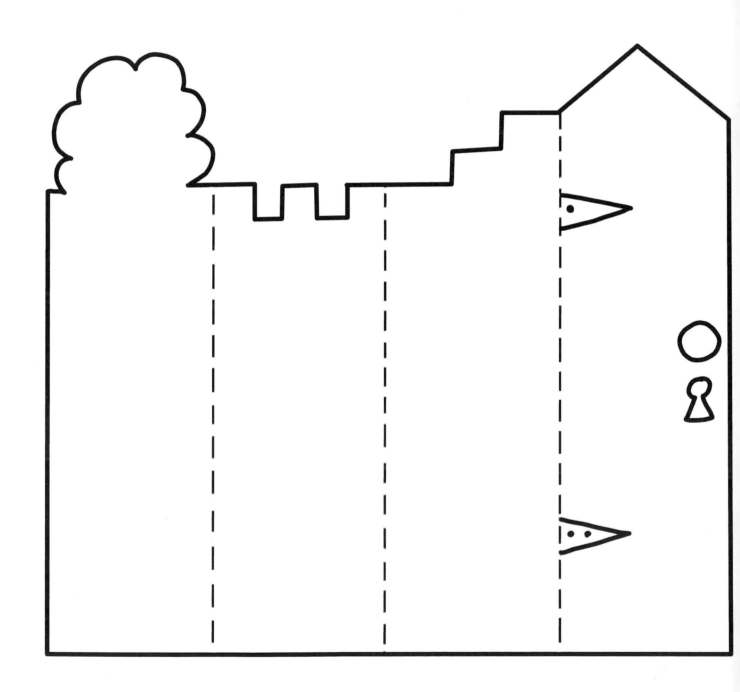

Photocopiable   **Knowledge and understanding of the world**

Make Teddy dance

Cut out the teddy parts and fix Teddy together.

SCHOLASTIC

A busy day

Saturday morning at Grandma's house. Tom could hear Gran, pottering in the kitchen. 🎼 He rushed down the stairs. 🎼

'Bin day today. You can help me sort the rubbish,' said Gran. She went through the kitchen door into the garage and Tom followed her. Gran pushed the outside garage door upwards, it stopped at the top with a loud clank. 🎼

Gran pointed four rubbish boxes out to Tom. 'Glass in that one,' she said, 'but be careful. Paper in that one. Metal in that one. And plastic in the last one. Now you have a look around and see what you can find.'

First, Tom looked for glass. He found a jam jar, a fish-paste jar and a bottle that had once had Grandma's special bath bubbles in. He placed them very carefully in the glass box. 🎼

Next, Tom found the tins. There were some tins from Puddy-Cat's food, a tin from the beans he had for his tea last night, and some Coke cans. Tom put the tins carefully in the metal box. 🎼

'Lots of old papers!' said Gran cheerfully. She bustled across to the paper box with a pile of newspapers. Tom collected up the old envelopes and letters that Gran didn't want any more, as well as some holiday brochures and a pile of screwed-up paper from the waste-paper bin. Into the paper box it all went. 🎼

Last thing of all was the plastic.

'There's a washing-up bottle here,' said Gran, 'and some plastic shopping bags.'

'And look what I've found!' said Tom. 'A margarine tub and some yoghurt pots.' He put them all into the plastic box. 🎼

'Right,' said Gran, 'now we have to put the boxes out at the top of the path.'

Tom carried the heavy paper box out to the pavement. 🎼

The boxes were out just in time, for down the road came the bin lorry, 🎼 with the bin men clinging to it like monkeys.

When they got by Gran's house, they all jumped off the lorry and shouted ''Morning!'' to Tom and Gran, then they began to pick up the boxes one by one and hurl all the rubbish into special containers. 🎼

Just as they waved goodbye to the bin men, it started to rain. 🎼

'Quick!' said Gran and they both ran as fast as they could 🎼 into the garage and slammed the door down 🎼 behind them.

Irene Yates

Spot the technology

Talk about the picture.

After 100 years

Talk about the picture.

Photocopiable

Knowledge and understanding of the world

My certificate

I can _____

Signed: _____

Dated: _____

Well done!

Town or country? (page 63), Word books (page 64)

Tale of two mice

A Country Mouse once invited a friend of his, who lived in town, to come and stay with him for a while. The Town Mouse soon arrived for his visit. Now, the Country Mouse ate simple country food like bread and cheese, beans and bacon. This was all he had, and he was happy to share it with his friend. When the Town Mouse saw the food, he turned up his nose. 'Really,' he said, 'I can't understand how you can eat food like this!' He patted his friend on the shoulder. 'I suppose I shouldn't have expected anything else in the country. Come and stay with me in town. I'll show you what proper food is. Just spend a week with me, and you'll wonder how you ever put up with this country life.'

The Country Mouse wondered if his friend might be right, so he agreed to go to town.

Next day, the two mice set off. When they arrived, the Town Mouse said, 'You must be hungry after the journey.' He set about making a meal. He laid out a wonderful feast for the Country Mouse. There was honey and raisins, figs, cake and all sorts of other wonderful things. The Country Mouse had never seen anything like it.

'Tuck in,' said his friend, and the two mice began to eat.

As he ate the delicious food, the Country Mouse thought of his life back in the country. 'What a poor time I have there,' he thought to himself. 'My friend has so much better a time here.'

No sooner had he thought this, than a loud barking noise began, making the Country Mouse shiver with fright.

'What on earth is that?' he asked the Town Mouse, in a shaky voice.

'Don't worry! It's just the dogs of the house. They do that all the time.'

Just then, the door opened and two huge dogs came bounding in. The mice ran for their lives.

When they were safe and had got their breath back, the Country Mouse looked at his friend. 'You may have plenty of wonderful food here,' he said, 'but at least I can eat my simple food in peace. I prefer my country life. I can live in safety there without fear.'

And he set off home, back to the countryside he loved.

Jillian Harker

Photocopiable   **Knowledge and understanding of the world**

Where can you find them?

Cut out the pictures and stick them in your word book.

Where do you live?

Talk about these homes.

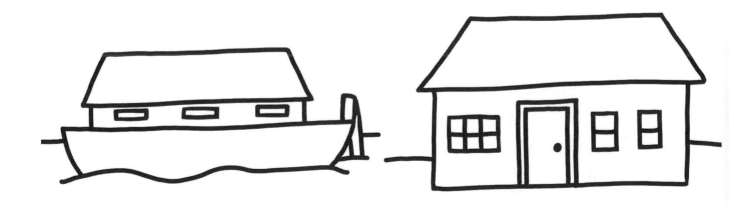

Photocopiable   **Knowledge and understanding of the world**

Spicy salsa

Ingredients
8 tomatoes (skinned, seeded and chopped into small cubes)

½ medium red onion (chopped finely)

I clove of garlic (crushed)

I tablespoon of freshly squeezed lime or lemon juice

I mild green chilli pepper (seeded and very finely chopped)

salt and pepper

What to do
Mix all the ingredients together in a bowl and chill in the fridge for about an hour.

The coming of Raven

Long ago, before the world began, there was only darkness. Then Raven, the Father of Life, made the earth. But he could not see the mountains, trees or seas, because everything was hidden in darkness.

Suddenly Raven saw a rock shining on the ground. He grabbed it in his claws and threw it into the sky. The rock was the sun. It lit up the earth.

As Raven looked at the things he had made, a plant popped open, and out fell the first Inuit man. The man was cold, hungry and lonely. So Raven made animals to provide the man with food and clothes. But he made the man promise not to kill any more animals than he really needed. Then Raven made a woman to keep the man company.

As time went on, the man and woman had children, and grandchildren. But the more people there were, the more animals they hunted, and the more they took from the earth. Raven was angry that the Inuit had forgotten their promise. But the people did not care. So Raven took a bag made from reindeer skin, flew up into the sky and stuffed the sun into the bag. The whole world fell back into darkness.

Sometimes, Raven would uncover the sun for a few days, feeling sorry for the Inuit. When he opened the bag, he showed the fiery rock to his son, Raven Boy, who was fascinated by the sun. He wanted to look at it more closely, so he tried to open the bag while his father was sleeping. But his father woke up, and Raven Boy ran away with the bag to the other side of the universe.

Now there was no sunshine at all, and the people on earth cried out, 'Please save us, Raven! Give us back the sun!' Then Raven called out to Raven Boy, 'Bring back the sun! Without it, the world I made will die.'

When he heard his father, Raven Boy ripped the bag open and flung the sun across the sky. But Raven wanted the Inuit people to remember what darkness was like and never forget their promise again. So he made day change into night and summer into winter. In this way, the Inuit were reminded to look after the world properly. They kept their promise. They respected all animals, and they honoured Raven, the creator of the earth.

Jillian Harker

Knowledge and understanding of the world